This is number two hundred and seventeen in the
second numbered series of the
Miegunyah Volumes
made possible by the
Miegunyah Fund
established by bequests
under the wills of
Sir Russell and Lady Grimwade.

'Miegunyah' was Russell Grimwade's home
from 1911 to 1955
and Mab Grimwade's home
from 1911 to 1973.

The Contemporary Australian Writers Series explores and articulates the significance of select Australian writers' literary works.

Contributors to the series act as both guide and critic, illuminating how literary works make and remake worlds—reimagining histories and futures, communities and institutions, families and homes. In doing so, the series recognises the unique role of the artist in shaping our perception of the world around us and, in the act of reading and critique, ourselves.

The series brings to the fore a public discussion of the value of the local in an international literary culture, and celebrates those writers whose work has moved us, enlightened us and surprised us.

Murnane

CONTEMPORARY AUSTRALIAN WRITERS

Murnane

Emmett Stinson

THE MIEGUNYAH PRESS

THE MIEGUNYAH PRESS
An imprint of Melbourne University Publishing Limited
Level 1, 715 Swanston Street, Carlton, Victoria 3053, Australia
mup-contact@unimelb.edu.au
www.mup.com.au

First published 2023

Cover design by Evi O. Studio
Text design and typesetting by Cannon Typesetting
Printed in Australia by McPherson's Printing Group

NATIONAL LIBRARY OF AUSTRALIA
A catalogue record for this book is available from the National Library of Australia

ISBN 9780522879469 (paperback)
ISBN 9780522879476 (ebook)

Series Editor: Melinda Harvey

MIX
Paper | Supporting responsible forestry
FSC® C001695

For Felix

Contents

Introduction: Gerald Murnane's Homemade World 1
Barley Patch and the Problem of Writing 20
The Author Is Absent: *A History of Books* 40
A Million Windows and the Implied Author 54
The Text Ends at This Point: *Border Districts* 71
Conclusion: Gerald Murnane's Late Style 84
Late Recognition: An Interview with Gerald Murnane 108
Notes 121
Bibliography 128
Acknowledgments 133

Introduction: Gerald Murnane's Homemade World

Very little happens in Gerald Murnane's fiction. In his debut novel, *Tamarisk Row* (1974), young Clement Killeaton sits in his backyard in Bassett—a fictionalised version of Bendigo—pretending that his marbles are racehorses. Adrian Sherd, the teenage protagonist of his second book, *A Season on Earth* (1976/2019)*, fantasises about US film stars, idealises a young girl that he is too afraid to speak to on his train ride to school, and briefly joins a monastery before giving up his vocation. Murnane's third and most famous novel, *The Plains* (1982), is about a young filmmaker who travels to regional Australia seeking funding from a rich patron; he receives patronage, but fails to make his film. There is little in the way of conventional plotting: no rising action, no conflict, no dramatic tension, no resolution. Neither do these novels

* Murnane's second novel, *Lifetime on Clouds* (1976) was republished in its full and complete version with the original title, *A Season on Earth* in 2019. This book will refer to the latter as Murnane's second novel.

feature extensive casts of characters. Instead, we encounter the thoughts and experiences of his protagonists, who are loners and daydreamers. The major conflicts in these novels occur within the protagonists' minds: *Tamarisk Row*, for example, is named after the imaginary community of horse-breeders and jockeys that Clement invents in his backyard marble game, which becomes as richly detailed as the nominal 'reality' of his life in Bassett.

Murnane's books stage a conflict between his protagonists' complex and satisfying imaginary worlds and the external world of experience. Murnane finds great humour in his protagonists' inability to resolve the two. As Imre Salusinszky has argued, Murnane's novels dramatise 'the relation of the individual mind to the reality confronting it'[1]. It is obvious that Adrian Sherd's intricate if strangely naïve sexual fantasies of film stars don't augur well for taking on the clerical collar. The unnamed film-maker's inability to complete his film is intentionally ridiculous: he never even attempts his work, because he becomes so absorbed in contemplating the ineffable nature of the Plains. And yet, these characters' failures are not simply a set-up for an ironic punchline. This is because Murnane's work takes imaginary realms very seriously. For this reason. J.M. Coetzee has described Murnane as 'a radical idealist'.[2] The second half of *Tamarisk Row* depicts the lives of the breeders and racers in the imaginary marble community of Tamarisk Row as if they were real. The filmmaker's desire to capture the Plains never really abates, because the process of imagining his unfilmable film becomes as important as making it. Adrian Sherd abandons the monastery, but his vocation towards something remains: he builds an almost monastic cell in the shed behind his parents' house where he quite literally hides from the world. The problem for these characters is not their rich inner worlds, but that these worlds remain incommensurate with the absolute fixity of external reality.

The Murnanian protagonist struggles because he (it's always and only a him) cannot adequately communicate his internal world to others. The crucial example in Murnane's early writing is Adrian Sherd's unrequited love for a girl that he spots on a train, his so-called Earth Angel. Adrian is so taken with this girl that he intentionally boards the same carriage for months, and—by spying on a notebook of hers—learns that her name is Denise McNamara. He considers introducing himself, but instead consults a phonebook to learn her address, and imagines writing to her parents to express his romantic intentions. Adrian remains unaware that his actions are creepy or worse. Such ironic depictions of unrequited love are hardly new in literature. Readers of *La Vita Nuova* will know that Dante barely spoke to Beatrice. James Joyce's 'Araby' (1914), tells a similar story, though the narrator understands his own foolishness far more quickly than Adrian (and 'Araby' almost certainly influenced Murnane given that one of his narrators calls Joyce 'the greatest of prose writers'[3]).

The Murnanian protagonist differs from most sufferers of unreturned affection. Adrian quickly loses interest in the real Denise, subsuming himself in complex daydreams of a future life with an imaginary version of her. *A Season on Earth* details their fantasy courtship and eventual break-up over a hundred pages, all of which occurs within Adrian's mind.

This imagined relationship seems ridiculous, but it is arguably the paradigmatic relationship within Murnane's fiction. As Samantha Trayhurn has noted, Murnane's description of the actual events that inspired the novel also suggest that the made-up relationship eclipsed the real one: after 'conversing for two or three weeks' the boy finds himself 'so ill at ease that he can't recall the details of their conversations' and decides to end his pursuit.[4] Murnane's characters repeatedly articulate a desire for an intense shared understanding that is wordless. The story 'Stone Quarry', for example, depicts a bizarre writer's retreat called Waldo (a punning reference to the real writer's retreat, Yaddo, and the author of 'Self-Reliance' (1841), Ralph Waldo Emerson) that strictly enforces a monastic policy of silence:

> The theory behind the vow of silence is that talk—even serious, thoughtful talk or talk about writing itself—drains away the writer's most precious resource, which is the belief that he or she is the solitary witness to an inexhaustible profusion of images from which might be read all the wisdom of the world.[5]

For Murnane's characters, language remains necessary but a degradation of the internal world of images, which provide access to a deeper meaning. The external world may be comically uninterested in the protagonists' elaborate daydreams, but these rich internal worlds also contain an ineffable and self-sufficient truth that surpasses reality.

Wordless understanding becomes an idealised mode of communication even though it is impossible. For this reason, this ideal mode of communication can only occur between imaginary people; the ending of 'Stone Quarry' recounts this impossible situation, where communication is only possible when the narrator imagines 'a world in which the woman does not exist and neither do I'.[6] Elsewhere, Murnane has written about his 'Ideal Reader' who 'supervises most of' his writing; this Ideal Reader is an invisible, female 'entity' with 'a distinctive appearance' though she does not resemble any actually living person, who has not 'uttered so much as a syllable' to Murnane, even though she seems somehow fond of him.[7] While the Ideal Reader does not speak—just like the characters in 'Stone Quarry'—she does communicate: Murnane states that he understands what she wants in the way that one intuits the 'demands of certain silent personages in dreams'.[8] This figure, who Murnane sometimes deems his 'Patroness', also recalls the literal patron of *The Plains* who supports the nameless filmmaker. I suspect that many readers—including me—might not know how to feel about the Ideal Reader, which seems like a strange mysticism (Murnane himself invokes Robert Graves's writings on his muse in comparison), or perhaps even an aestheticised Marist theology; Brigid Rooney has argued that Murnane's 'yearnings towards ideal women' are shaped by his 'suburban Catholicism'.[9] But the 'Ideal Reader' emphasises that imaginary, wordless relationships are a vital form of relation for Murnane.

Murnane's writing playfully slips between fiction and autobiography. As Anthony Uhlmann has noted, Murnane's works 'cannot easily be classified as "novels"', and often shift between 'the essay form and the fictional form'.[10] Shannon Burns has argued that Murnane's writing 'appears to be increasingly truthful and revealing' and functions effectively like autobiography, despite employing a set of 'distancing devices' that emphasise his work's fictionality.[11] Murnane has variously described the relationship of reality and truth in his writing. Sometimes he describes his work as 'true fiction'. At other points, he has appropriated Wayne Booth's concept of the 'implied author'—a complicated literary-critical concept that can only be fully understood in relation to specific problems of interpretation generated by the twentieth-century movement known as the New Criticism; for Murnane, however, the implied author refers to the fictional avatars of himself that narrate his works, and who are separate from the living person who wrote the books. Murnane employs these avatars to fictionalise and transform his autobiographical experiences: while readers frequently wonder to what degree Murnane's characters resemble him, he prefers responding with 'evasive answers'.[12] Murnane's writing hybridises fiction, essay, and memoir in ways that anticipate contemporary autofiction, and it can be hard to predict what is real and what is fictional. For example, I asked Murnane about the writing technique described in the short story, 'In Far Fields', in which individual sentences are placed in folders of different colors. This seems wholly consistent with Murnane's well-known tendencies to archive his writing in filing cabinets, but he looked at me confusedly, before saying, 'Oh, I made that up.' Louis Klee, however, has more recently noted that the five-point diagram which is discussed as a compositional system in the same story has been employed by the real Murnane both for his writing and his teaching.[13]

The protagonists of Murnane's works all resemble the real Gerald Murnane. He did, as a child, play a complex horseracing game in Bendigo with marbles. I have seen these same marbles, which now sit in two medium-sized jars on his desk. In the story 'The Interior of Gaaldine' from *Emerald Blue*, a character describes his complex fictional horseracing game set in two imaginary countries named New Eden and New Arcady. But the real Murnane plays a virtually identical game. I have seen part of this 'Antipodean Archive', which he has described as containing 'a thousand pages of typescripts, manuscripts, maps, charts, diagrams, lists, and sketches describing the organization, administration and day-to-day running of horse-racing', as well as the detailed 'results of several hundred races' that he began recording in 1985.[14] The Antipodean Archive is, for all intents and purposes, a role-playing game: instead of dice, he randomly selects telephone numbers from an old phone directory to determine the outcome of races. He creates characters for the various racers and owners, and even cuts out faces from magazines and newspapers (many of whom are celebrities, though Murnane is often unaware of who they are), which are 'assigned' to his various imaginary characters. He assiduously collates this material in three-ring binders.

Similarly, we know that Gerald Murnane, as a young man, developed a complex infatuation with a young girl on a train he never spoke to, and that—like Adrian Sherd—he briefly embarked upon a vocation in the priesthood by entering a monastery. His room in Goroke immediately reminded me of Adrian Sherd's backyard shed: the spare, small, white-walled room contains his famous filing cabinets (where he has kept records of much of his life and holds many unpublished writings), a selection of books, his marbles, his violin, a poster of the winners of the Melbourne Cup and a few other prized possessions. In a small folder on top of one cabinet he has organised his will and other papers that will be necessary for his children after his death (Murnane has been 'described by my wife and several friends as the most organised person they have ever known'[15]). He sleeps on a small swag that he stows every evening on top of his filing cabinets. It is a singular dwelling: half monk's cell and half cabinet of wonders. Mark Binelli, in a profile of Murnane for *The New York Times Magazine*, has described his room as 'a blend of fanatical organization and claustrophobia, as if a squatter had taken over a secluded wing of a research library'.[16] Murnane encourages this comparison in his poem 'A Cistercian Life', when he notes the unusual deprivations of his way of living 'without radio, TV, telephone or computer' and states that 'I have made no vow of silence but I haven't spoken since yesterday when I called at the store'.[17]

Murnane's unusual living conditions are not the result of penury or desperation, but rather of disposition and familial duty. He still owns the house in the northern Melbourne suburb of Macleod, which appears in many of his fictional works. Even his much-discussed move to Goroke, which occurred shortly after the death of his wife of forty years, was not motivated by a desire to be reclusive; as a writer who's known Murnane for decades said to me, 'You know he's not a hermit, right?' Goroke, with a population of under two hundred, is in no danger of becoming a tourist attraction though Murnane is not the only recent arrival: when I asked him what motivates people to move there, he jokingly suggested it was often caused by the opposite of winning the lottery. While Murnane has fictionalised the move to Goroke in his final novel, *Border Districts* (2017), he offered a more straightforward explanation in an interview with Shannon Burns: 'One of the main reasons I came to Goroke was so that I could look after my son, at the age of seventy. I'm his father and I can't avoid helping him'.[18] He has discussed the matter further:

> After Catherine's death, Melbourne didn't feel like home anymore, and I thought, 'I can live anywhere now. I don't have to live here.' Anyway, I leased the place to one of my sons and here I am. And Giles, my older son, came with me.[19]

Although it is rarely acknowledged, Murnane's fiction often foregrounds caring for children and other domestic responsibilities in a manner that is unusual for authors of his generation. For example, 'The Battle of Acosta Nu' offers a complex reflection on a real-life situation in which Murnane's son ended up in hospital. Another story from this period, 'When the Mice Failed to Arrive', again finds a Murnane-like narrator caring for his asthmatic son while a thunderstorm approaches. But the move to Goroke also reflects Murnane's willingness to follow his own sense of how to live, rather than concerning himself with social conventions. The choice to sleep on a swag in a spare room in a tiny, remote town does seem strange, but so does pursuing a forty-year career writing impossible-to-categorise literary fiction that has never sold well and often provoked confusion among critics. Murnane is a singular writer, and an unusual person.

In his essay 'The Breathing Author' Murnane recounts his belief that what someone 'cannot do or has never done' is more revealing than 'what he has or wants to do'.[20] Murnane has not flown in an airplane, has 'no sense of smell' and 'a rudimentary sense of taste', has never 'owned a television', has 'watched few films', has never willingly attended 'any art gallery or museum', has 'never learned to swim', has never used 'a library catalogue', has never operated a camera, and has 'never touched' a 'computer or fax machine or mobile telephone'.[21] While Murnane has more recently become an intermittent user of mobile phones (he turns it on only for specific periods of the day and communicates via epistle-length text messages), he still has not used a computer and does not browse the internet, though friends print out online reviews and essays on his work, almost all of which he reads. What is unique about Murnane is the way that he has managed to craft his fictional works out of his intentionally limited experiences.

Murnane's life—in many respects—seems relatively uneventful if not conventional. Hugh Kenner has described the work of a group of US modernist writers as a 'homemade cosmopolitanism' that sought 'to perfect some affirmation of the local'.[22] Kenner's point was that, unlike much of the highly conceptual European literature of the early twentieth century, US literature trained a cosmopolitan eye on local detail, seeking avant-garde energies in what was at hand. The most famous example of this is William Carlos Williams' *Paterson* (1946–58), whose five books traverse the history of Paterson,

New Jersey—a city that few would have previously considered a likely site for an epic poem. Gerald Murnane, while not a US modernist, shares a sensibility with these writers: his work, rather being limited by the narrow horizons of his experience, uses those limitations to create a distinctive and unusual mode of fiction: a localised form of an international, avant-garde tradition.

Murnane was born in Coburg, a northern suburb of Melbourne in 1939. Owing to his father's frequent and significant gambling debts, the young Murnane moved often between houses and even regions of Melbourne including Bendigo and the Western District. Much of his fiction draws on his experience of growing up in a working-class Catholic family in the 1940s and 1950s, and vividly though critically examines the strict social prohibitions of this upbringing, particularly around sexuality, the shame of the body, and gender relations. Murnane has infamously never travelled outside Australia and rarely travelled beyond his home state of Victoria. He has left mainland Australia only once, crossing the Bass Strait on a ferry to visit Tasmania for a conference. Murnane briefly trained for the priesthood, and then worked as a clerk at the Royal Mint in Melbourne. He studied to become a primary school teacher at Toorak Teacher's College, and taught for eight years. In 1969, as a mature-aged student, he graduated from the University of Melbourne with a Bachelor of Arts in English and Arabic. During the 1970s, he was an editor, publications officer, freelance writer, and stay-at-home carer for his children. He published his first two novels before securing a position as a Lecturer in Fiction Writing at Prahran College of Advanced

Education, which would later become Deakin University. He worked in this role until his retirement from both teaching and writing in 1995.

The humble origins of Murnane's work and his prevailing interest in specific under-represented localities in Australia—including regional towns like Bendigo and Warrnambool, as well as many working-class northern suburbs of Melbourne—remain at odds with his surprisingly divisive local reception. While his first novel was a finalist for The Age Book of the Year Award, his books have rarely won literary awards. He is certainly the most lauded, living Australian author never to have won the Miles Franklin award, arguably the most prestigious national literary prize; he has only made the shortlist once. His final novel, *Border Districts,* won the Prime Minister's Literary Award for Fiction in 2018, his only win of a major Australian literary prize aside from several recognitions for lifetime achievement, such as the Patrick White Award. He has also won multiple state-based literary awards. Nonetheless, Murnane's third novel, *The Plains,* earned him an early cult following. Even after this, he has often received viciously negative reviews from critics of all kinds. For example, his next book, the collection of interconnected short stories, *Landscape with Landscape* (1985), was attacked by the conservative commentator, Gerard Windsor in his review, 'Flawed Fiction from a Local, Modish Messiah', for being too fashionably experimental. But reviewers on the left similarly criticised its 'post-modern paralysis' and allegedly conservative cultural politics.[23]

In the early 2000s, Professor Ken Gelder, an Australian literary scholar at the University of Melbourne whose criticism draws on approaches influenced by the Birmingham School of Cultural Studies, would label Murnane a 'monomaniacal Australian Tory modernist'.[24] Gelder's description is obviously intended as a pejorative, but it is essentially accurate: Murnane's obsessive recording and archiving of his personal experiences and his extended devotion to writing and publishing experimental literary work with little obvious commercial potential are monomaniacal in some sense. Gelder even notes that 'Monomania is especially suited to the formalism of literary projects' because 'it creates a space or a practice that is autonomous, internally coherent, and with its special rules and logics'.[25] Gelder equates this artistic monomania with exclusive and elitist spaces, such as an 'exclusive club' or an 'orchard or a garden of one's own',[26] but in Murnane's case, it is hard not to compare his particular aesthetic monomania with the rigorous order of his unrarified monkish chamber in Goroke. Murnane has obsessively catalogued his own experiences, but this cataloguing may be motivated by much simpler desires for understanding: as Murnane told Mark Binelli, he has enormous difficulty comprehending human behaviour: 'I don't know what anyone is thinking … People are a mystery to me'.[27]

Australian critics have often taken a harsh view of Murnane's work, as Joseph Steinberg notes, on the basis of its alleged 'self-centredness, facile fussiness, conservatism and elitism'.[28] To what degree are these charges substantively correct? Murnane described himself to me as effectively apolitical. The narrator of *A History of Books* (2012) similarly states that he had 'never felt drawn to any political party' and 'never signed any petition or any document protesting … seeming injustice',[29] though this rejection of left-wing protest seems politically significant. So too, does Murnane's long friendship with Imre Salusinszky—a former academic who has worked as a journalist at such conservative publications as *Quadrant* and *The Australian*, as well as serving as media director for the conservative premier of New South Wales, Mike Baird. There is little obvious political comment in Murnane's fiction, but his recent book of poems does veer into partisan terrain. In *Green Shadows and Other Poems*, the poems criticise a 'certain kind of atheist', gently chastise the views of a former 'Marxist colleague of mine', note Murnane's 'life-long doubt/as to the wisdom of working for change', and describe climate change as a 'cranky theory about the weather'.[30] None of these positions would be particularly surprising for close readers of Murnane's fiction; his criticism of materialist understandings of the world has been explicit since his extended attack on the biological basis of cognition in *The Plains* (a character pointedly criticises the idea that the brain could produce the complex experience of consciousness). While these positions do seem broadly if idiosyncratically conservative, their larger ideological coordinates are harder to locate.

Critical political readings of Murnane's work have rarely been either specific or substantiated; Salzman and Gelder's claim that Murnane's fiction presents a 'sense of landscape as somehow virginal and fulfilled only through pastoral settlement'[31] ignores Murnane's short story 'Land Deal' (1980), which, as Nicholas Birns argues, presents 'a searing depiction of the white settlement of Australia as a nightmare from which Aboriginal dreamers are determined to awake'.[32] Murnane's pastoral landscapes are complexly ironised, as in *The Plains*, in ways that do not simply idealise settlement. In his memoir, *Something for the Pain,* Murnane notes that, during his time working at Deakin University, he often felt isolated from academic colleagues who might be discussing a recent documentary from the national public broadcaster, when he had no interest in such things.[33] Murnane's interests—such as horseracing—do not overlap with those of most urban intellectuals in Australia. Part of Murnane's perceived conservatism may simply reflect these differences, though the ultimate release of his archives will inevitably make Murnane's political commitments much clearer, and perhaps uncomfortably so. Regardless, the lauded Australian poet Les Murray articulated far more explicitly right-wing views without damaging his literary standing. I suspect that, in Murnane's case, his perceived conservatism alongside his refusal of realist conventions marks him as a target of criticism in an Australian literary culture that often still skews towards an aesthetic orientation that Patrick White decried as 'the dreary, dun-coloured offspring of journalistic realism'.[34] It does not help that Murnane has often been outspoken in his criticisms of Australian publishing and literary institutions in ways that have not endeared him to influential tastemakers. Finally, there is the issue of the representation of women in Murnane's work—a far more complicated and significant criticism, which I will address at length later.

Paul Genoni notes two observations frequently made about Murnane's work and its reception: 'that he has poor sales in Australia, and that he is more appreciated elsewhere'.[35] Murnane's work has found a receptive and almost unanimously positive international audience in the United States, the United

Kingdom, and Sweden, among others. He has been the subject of an extensive profile in *The New York Times Magazine* and essays by major overseas authors and critics in *The New Yorker* (twice, by Ben Lerner and Merve Emre, respectively), *The London Review of Books* (by Christian Lorentzen), *The New York Review of Books* (by J.M. Coetzee), and many others. His fiction is now published by such highly regarded publishers as Dalkey Archive Press, And Other Stories, and Farrar, Straus and Giroux overseas, and Giramondo and Text Publishing here in Australia. This late career resurgence is perhaps even more unlikely, because—in 1995—Murnane decided to give up writing entirely and did not publish another work of fiction for fourteen years. Since his un-retirement, Murnane has published three novels, a novella and stories, a memoir, a book of poems, a book of essays, a volume of his collected short stories, and a restored version of his second novel, which is nearly double the length of the original. This is in addition to eight book-length works of fiction and the collection of essays he published prior to 2009. The result is a significant bibliography that is highly self-referential. He says that he intends to write no more fiction and that he has published his final book, *Last Letter to a Reader*—a collection of essays examining own work book-by-book, including a chapter on this final book of essays itself. This book emphasises Murnane's desire to frame and shape his own literary legacy: he is technically the first author of a critical work about the complete oeuvre of Gerald Murnane.

This book will focus on Murnane's late novels, which comprise four works published between 2009 and 2017: *Barley Patch*, *A History of Books*, *A Million Windows*, and *Border*

Districts. Since these novels variously refer and respond to Murnane's early works of fiction, writing about them will also entail discussing his larger body of work. Murnane's fiction, as Anthony Uhlmann has suggested, can be roughly divided into three periods: 1) his first two novels, *Tamarisk Row* and *A Season on Earth,* which are written in third person, 2) the pre-break works of fiction written in first person from *The Plains* to *Emerald Blue,* and 3) the post-break fictions, which increasingly ruminate on questions of method.[36] This typology seems to make a nice argument for the existence of this book, which focuses on the post-break works, but the divisions in Murnane's work may not be so straightforward. For one, Murnane himself has railed against the notion that his body of work was planned in some coherent way, given that he had enormous difficulty publishing his work, and that his works themselves were often radically changed by publishers.

It is true, as Imre Salusinszky has noted, that Murnane's first two novels—*Tamarisk Row* and *A Season on Earth*—were written in the third person, while virtually all of his subsequent books are written in the first person. This claim, however, refers to the published versions of these books, and not the original manuscripts, which were markedly different. The earliest version of *The Plains* was a much longer manuscript titled *The Only Adam;* I suspect that this original version might be much closer to the style of *A Season on Earth* than the published version of *The Plains* is. Murnane's fourth book, *Landscape with Landscape,* has one story that clearly resembles *The Plains* ('The Battle of Acosta Nu'), but the rest of the book moves away from *The Plains'* philosophical allegory and resembles the autobiographically inflected fiction that characterises Murnane's later work. What *does* seem different in *Landscape with Landscape* is Murnane's increasing interest in metafictional games: each story in the book appears to contain the story before it, and the final narrator appears to be the author of all of these stories. These metafictional conceits are extended further in the 1988 novel, *Inland.* Murnane would publish two short story collections—*Velvet Waters* and *Emerald Blue*—before his retirement from writing in 1995. While these stories recall *Landscape with Landscape,* they also increasingly reflect back on his own methods of composition in a way similar to the post-break works. I am uncertain that there is any easy periodisation of Murnane's work, and such differentiation is further complicated by the fact that his writing so often refers back to itself.

There are, however, two key arguments for seeing the final four novels as being definitively different in a way that separates them from his earlier work. First, as Murnane himself has noted, the deep and singular support offered to him by Giramondo and its publisher, Ivor Indyk, has meant that—for the first time in his career—he knows that his work will be published in the form that he intended it. The final four works of fiction, unlike the first seven, are in *no way* 'mutilated versions'[37] of his intention. I have spoken to an editor of one of Murnane's post-break books who informed me that—of the dozens of works of fiction she has edited—Murnane's work had required the least intervention with only *two changes* being actioned across the entire manuscript. Second, these late works reflect back on Murnane's own writing to an extreme degree that feels deliberately summative. They remind me of two objects in Murnane's room in Goroke: his filing cabinets containing his personal archive, and his will and related documents organised in a folder for when dies. Murnane clearly cares about his literary and personal legacy, and, as I will argue, these late works of fiction serve a similar purpose: to complete, belatedly, his oeuvre and impose some final order on the more contingent and disordered conditions in which his early works were published. From this perspective, a study of Murnane's late fiction offers a unique insight into the way that he has chosen to refashion his own authorial career.

Barley Patch and the Problem of Writing

Gerald Murnane published no fiction between 1995 and 2009. *Barley Patch* was his first new work of fiction in fourteen years, and his first novel in twenty years, since *Inland*. The final story in *Emerald Blue* (1995), 'The Interior of Gaaldine', opens with the claim that it is a 'true account' of 'the evening when I decided to write no more fiction' and concludes with the line 'The text ends at this point'.[38] This story was intended to explain why Murnane gave up writing, though virtually no-one noticed this at the time. Murnane's 'break' from publishing, however, is more complicated than it seems: in *Barley Patch*, the narrator, who resembles Murnane, states that '[f]our years after I had stopped writing fiction, my seventh book of fiction [*Emerald Blue*] was published' in 1995.[39] So Murnane 'retired' from writing in 1991, except for 'three other pieces' he wrote to complete *Emerald Blue*.[40] As the novel implies, this decision was in some way motivated by his failure to finish a long manuscript, entitled *O, Dem Golden Slippers.* To complicate matters further, Murnane also published an essay collection, *Invisible Yet Enduring Lilacs* in 2005, which included at least one piece, 'The Breathing Author', written in 2001, for a conference on his work at the University of Newcastle in September that year. Moreover, the three short stories that accompany the titular novella in *A History of Books* (2012) were all published during the break in 2001–2, but perhaps these were initially intended to be memoir, rather than fiction. By Murnane's own contention, he has 'never tried to write fiction or non-fiction or anything in-between' and thus should have published 'all my pieces of writing as essays'.[41] Regardless, Murnane was surprisingly active for a 'retired' author. His retirement was incomplete in other ways, since he continued to write in various personal forms, but not for publication. But the partial nature of Murnane's retirement perhaps reflects how significant for him the decision to stop writing was, and it is the very question that *Barley Patch* begins with: '*Must I write?*'.[42]

Barley Patch's two parts are structured around thirteen of these discursive questions and prompts in italics. Some grow to nearly a paragraph in length. This form might recall the 'Ithaca' section of Joyce's *Ulysses*, which also alternates between quick questions and informative answers, but Joyce's encyclopedic, hypotactic style deploys a humorous excess of information, whereas *Barley Patch*'s 'answers' typically evade their questions and prompts:

> I would be willing to admit that I have not yet answered the impending question, but only if my hypothetical questioner

> would admit that a question can hardly be worth asking if its answer can be delivered in fewer than ten thousand words.[43]

Where 'Ithaca' expounds, *Barley Patch* withholds: the reader's curiosity about why Murnane stopped writing is comically deferred. Murnane's fiction often hovers in between sincere belief and laconic irony. Although Murnane himself has dismissed 'Ithaca' as a model for *Barley Patch*, they do share themes: 'Ithaca' draws on the form of the Catholic catechism, and *Barley Patch* foregrounds the young narrator's early Catholicism and brief attempt to undertake a vocation in the priesthood. The significance of having exactly 'thirteen' prompts is unclear: as Brigid Rooney notes, 'Whatever organises this division of material is not obvious'.[44] Murnane told me that the number had no meaning, but, given the novel's description of blasphemous parodies of church ritual, it may well be linked to the thirteen attendees of the last supper and the unlucky association of thirteen with Judas Iscariot.

While these prompts provide *Barley Patch* with an organising principle, it has no conventional plot. Part One takes up 175 of the novel's 265 pages, and begins with the narrator (who resembles Murnane) considering his decision to stop writing and reflecting on his early reading practices. The narrator then attempts to imagine the 'events that … resulted in my being conceived',[45] but focuses on his fraught relationship with his uncle, a lifelong bachelor who died of cancer. Here *Barley Patch* alludes to *Tristram Shandy,* in which the narrator recounts the story of his own birth with a focus on his eccentric uncle Toby. *Barley Patch* obliquely depicts the scene of his mother and father's first meeting, but this is only one narrative strand in a broader collage of memories and events, including his childhood awe at the mysteries of the Catholic tabernacle, his belief in his ghostly 'Patroness' who lives on a different plane of existence from him, his family's displeasure over the sexual content in his early novels, his aunt's failed vocation as a nun, his childhood preference for bright colours over sweets, and his experiences in group therapy as a young bachelor.

Part Two returns to the question of why the narrator gave up writing, focusing on the novel—*O, Dem Golden Slippers*—that he decided not to complete in 1991. Much of Part Two summarises key scenes from the unfinished novel, and arguably constitutes a revision of it. The narrator briefly discusses how the protagonist of that novel had decided to join the priesthood and then recounts a series of conversations among a group of people who met in a flat inhabited by a young unmarried couple, whose living together was potentially scandalous in Melbourne in the early 1960s. The narrator then ties together the name *O, Dem Golden Slippers* (a popular song that he used to listen to on his aunt's record player) with horseracing through the Golden Slipper Stakes, a race in which the winning horse was given a golden horseshoe. The recounting of *O, Dem Golden Slippers* is once again imbricated with memories, including a set of hallucinations the narrator experienced in the 1960s after being proscribed psilocybin as a psychiatric treatment.

Barley Patch seems to dwell on aesthetic concerns, but these fixations conceal great pathos, including the author's struggles with loneliness, isolation, and mental illness—all of which are recurrent themes in Murnane's work. It also charts a psychogeography: as Brigid Rooney notes, the novel takes place in 'the roughly triangular space between Melbourne, Bendigo, and Warrnambool' moving between 'the comfortable homes provided by the narrator's extended family, the more ramshackle homes provided by his debt-ridden, gambling father, and the places inhabited by the young [narrator] during his fitful and lonely early career'.[46] One aspect of Murnane's fiction rarely noted is its depiction of working-class characters and culture in mid-century Australia; though Murnane's vision is highly aestheticised, many of its allegedly aristocratic yearnings might be best understood as working-class idealisations of a better life. The visions of estates and manor houses are the dreams that might be associated with winning the lottery or having a horseracing tip pay off.

The diverse content of *Barley Patch* is leant force through the novel's opening question ('*Must I write?*'), but the question is not Murnane's. It comes from a passage in Rainer Maria Rilke's *Letters to a Young Poet*, which is quoted at length. This seemingly straightforward question branches in three temporal directions: 1) why did Murnane, in 1991, decide to give up writing? 2) why did Murnane begin writing in the first place? and 3) why is the narrator 'writing' this novel now? For both Murnane and Rilke, writing must have a specific purpose; as Rilke states in the same letter, a 'work of art is good if it has sprung from necessity'.[47] The letter could almost be a manifesto for Murnane's literary project:

> Therefore save yourself from these general themes and seek those which your own everyday life offers you; describe

> your sorrows and desires, passing thoughts and the belief in some sort of beauty—describe all these with loving quiet, humble sincerity, and use, to express yourself, the things in your environment, the images from your dreams, and the objects of your memory. If your daily life seems poor, do not blame it: blame yourself, tell yourself that you are not poet enough to call forth its riches … And even if you were in some prison the walls of which let none of the sounds of the world come to your senses—would you not then still have your childhood, that precious kingly possession, that treasure-house of memories? Turn your attention thither.[48]

Arguably all of Murnane's fiction immerses itself in the private experiences, memories, and dreams that Rilke discusses. Part of Murnane's achievement lies in his capacity to mythologise the seeming banal fascinations—fetishes, really—that reappear across works: marbles, horseracing, stained-glass windows, the beloved girl on the train who is never spoken to, fear of the ocean, and love for mostly level countryside with trees in the distance. But the correlations between this passage from Rilke and *Barley Patch* are even more direct. Murnane's discussion of a memory palace late in the novel directly alludes to Rilke's 'treasure-house of memories' and the imagined silent prison similarly recalls the frequent depictions within Murnane's book of monasteries and convents that enforce a rule of silence. All of this illustrates the complex influence of Rilke on *Barley Patch:* it simultaneously poses the question that prompts the novel, comprises a manifesto (in advance) of Murnane's own writing, and presents a thematic and generative formal template for the novel itself. The narrator follows Rilke's last suggestion by turning to Murnane's childhood experiences of reading.

If *Barley Patch* is a novel about writing, it is also very much a novel about reading. This deeply allusive novel refers both to Murnane's own works (published and unpublished) and a wide range of other sources, including Josephine Tey's *Brat Farrar*, Charles Kingsley's *Hereward the Wake* and *Westward Ho!*, *Emily* Brontë's *Wuthering Heights*, Louisa May Alcott's *Little Women*, Proust's *Remembrance of Things Past*, Sidney Hobson Courtier's *The Glass Spear*, Matthew Arnold's 'The Scholar-Gypsy' and 'The Forsaken Merman', William Allingham's 'The Fairies', Oliver Goldsmith's *The Deserted Village*, Thomas Hardy's *Tess of the d'Urbervilles*, Lawrence Sterne's *Tristram Shandy*, Thomas Merton's *Elected Silence*, the work of Thomas Aquinas, Claud Cockburn's *Bestseller*, Turgenev (on characters), Frances Yates's *The Art of Memory*, and, of course, Rilke's *Letters to a Young Poet*. Most of these references are packed into its opening third, after which the novel increasingly becomes invested in a series of shorter narrative scenes that are placed together in a montage.

Reading—especially forms of naïve reading—are foregrounded in *Barley Patch*. Merve Emre has been one of the few scholars to acknowledge 'how important bad reading is to the history of literature', and has argued that it is essential to explore its 'logics of action' and relationships to key institutions of literacy in the twentieth century.[49] Emre argues that a new class of 'paraliterary readers' emerged midcentury, whose seemingly 'untutored scenes of literacy' often disguised 'complicated modes of reading'.[50] Emre positions paraliterary readers as the opposite of the 'good readers' imagined by educational institutions, including the 'close reader' who was idealised by the New Critics,' and the 'critical reader' imagined by 'literary theorists'[51]; in both instances 'good' reading is associated with the methods of academic literary criticism. Despite the seemingly avant-garde nature of Murnane's writing, he has routinely associated himself with paraliterary reading practices and unequivocally contrasted his own reading practices with academic literary criticism.

Murnane has articulated a strong dislike of literary criticism throughout his work. His early decision to enter the priesthood resulted from his desire to avoid attending university, as his family expected, because he found 'the *study* of English distasteful, hateful' and 'wholly confusing' despite having won 'the prize for English Literature' in high school.[52] Murnane is a classic example of Emre's 'paraliterary' reader, whose economic need for formal education brought him into direct contact with academic modes of criticism. Murnane elucidates his struggles in the subject 'English One', taught as a night school class for teachers seeking a tertiary qualification at the University of Melbourne in 1964. Murnane and his classmates were part of this new class of 'hundreds of thousands of bad readers conscripted' into institutional forms of criticism by the demands of paraliterary employment.[53] Murnane notes his distress in thinking of the time he and others 'wasted' on 'a pointless and probably impossible task'; most of his fellow students simply wanted 'a degree' and to 'get back to real life'.[54]

Murnane objects not only to the utility of academic criticism, but also to its content. He was 'no trouble-maker' and simply wanted to learn 'the orthodox view of each set text' and to 'paraphrase that view', but he could not please his Leavisite instructor.[55] Of Leavis's criticism, Murnane's assessment is brutal: 'What little I understood repelled me; the rest made no sense'.[56] The lectures sought to turn him and his fellow students into critics by assessing literary works on criteria 'promulgated' by a 'narrow-minded and truculent splitter of hairs in Cambridge'.[57] At the Goroke conference, which I attended, Murnane handed out copies of one of his English exams, and explained how pointless its questions were, perhaps as a warning to his would-be critics. In *Barley Patch,* the narrator explicitly counterpoises his literary tastes with those of academic literary critics, noting his worry that studying English at university might stop him from writing the kind of 'fiction that I hoped to write'.[58] Murnane politely interrogated my own motives for writing this book, asking 'What do you think you're doing when you're writing criticism? What do you think you're doing when you're writing a critical account of an author?' From his perspective, literary criticism on his writing seems irrelevant, because he already knows what he is doing.

Several years earlier, I had given a paper at the conference on Murnane's work at the Goroke Golf Club. Murnane had no interest in it—but why would he? As Mark Binelli recounts, Murnane had 'positioned himself behind the bar and flipped through a newspaper, half-listening to presentations with titles like "Intention and Retrospective Revision in Gerald Murnane's *Border Districts*"', which was, of course, my talk. What Binelli does not say, though I remember it well, is that—about a minute into the paper—Murnane, who I had never previously spoken to or corresponded with, left the room and sat outside. As a critic of Murnane's work, I have never doubted my place. Nevertheless, Murnane was entirely affable and polite to all in attendance in Goroke, and even tended bar during lunch. For Murnane, academic criticism does not address the most important experiences of reading from childhood onwards, because it fails to acknowledge that books can have 'more power over us than most of the things happening around us in the world', that characters in books can feel 'closer to us than most of the persons in the world', or that a reader might 'fall in love' with characters in the same way that one falls in love with real people.[59] These are classic examples of 'bad' reading, which fall under Emre's category of 'emotive' paraliterary readers who often seek love in fictional forms: 'a vision of love that exists more powerfully, more perfectly, in another space and time, and thus avoids its material realities'.[60] Such forms of immaterial readerly love are repeatedly glorified in Murnane's writing and seem to coincide, for him, with the value of literature itself.

Murnane explores his paraliterary childhood in *Barley Patch*. Instead of reading children's books, he preferred 'adult's books' that were borrowed 'from a circulating library' and returned the next week before he had 'read more than a few pages'.[61] Murnane outs himself as a bad reader here, because his reading was almost always partial. The only other way he could access reading materials (his parents did not own books) was in a serialised form in then-popular magazines, such as *Argosy* and *The Australian Journal*. Whereas digital technology has now produced an excess of available content, Murnane's early experiences of reading are marked by scarcity. It is perhaps surprising that Australia's most celebrated experimental or highbrow author locates his first reading experiences in popular fiction titles, such as Josephine Tey's *Brat Farrar* and Sidney Hobson Courtier's *The Glass Spear.* These works of popular fiction are very different from Murnane's own writing, but he creatively repurposed them for his own ends; he would take from this early reading the 'details worthy to be included in the scenery that I needed to have always at the back of my mind'.[62] These early fictions provided raw materials that could be transformed in Murnane's mind later, and he could occupy the 'gaps in the narrative' in certain stories and even insert himself as a 'ghostly fictional character' into the backgrounds of stories to interact with other characters and landscapes.[63] In doing this, Murnane is engaging in some of the most naïve readerly speculations—imagining what the characters do outside of the main plot of the novel or wondering what happens after the main narrative ends. These are classic examples of paraliterary reading, which are leant an unexpected substance by Murnane's metafictional approaches.

The narrator's ghostly haunting of fictional texts mirrors the many spectral presences that populate *Barley Patch*, including the narrator's mother's ghost story about Old Eric, the dead girl Bridget from Allingham's 'The Fairies', the mysterious and secretive Huldah from *The Glass Spear*, and the imaginary ethereal 'Patroness' who seems to be the same as Murnane's Ideal Reader. These figures also recall the opening section of *Wuthering Heights*, a touchstone for Murnane, in which Mr Lockwood has a vision of Catherine's ghost trying to break through a windowpane; the narrator of *Barley Patch* later describes himself as a 'ghost-character' who is 'barely visible'.[64] As Murnane has noted in an interview with Antoni Jach, '*Barley Patch* is full of references to things existing on the other side of works of art. And imaginary places'.

Huldah from *The Glass Spear* forms the bridge that links Murnane's early reading with his writing. Huldah is a recluse who has lived since childhood on a large homestead in 'the most remote room', which is locked and has its blinds 'always drawn in the windows'.[65] She remains a mystery to the other residents, who do not know why she chooses to live 'in secret'.[66] Huldah is a typically Murnanian figure: his writing repeatedly depicts recluses who choose to stay in their rooms rather than interacting with the outside world. But Huldah also inspired Murnane to write his first short story when he was eleven or twelve years old, which was 'set on a large rural property in inland Tasmania'.[67] It was about a young man and woman who lived in distant rooms in a large homestead whose floorplan resembled 'an upper-case H'; the protagonist was also named Gerald, while the woman had the name of an older girl from Murnane's school who he had 'spent much time observing' even though she was probably 'unaware' of his existence.[68] In Murnane's childhood story we can already see key features of his later fiction: reclusive figures, large manor houses, and unrequited and unacknowledged love. The narrator of *Barley Patch* notes that he wrote in secret, hiding his story under the floor in his bedroom. When his mother subsequently found the story, she asked a series of questions that Murnane would later receive at author events, including whether his fiction was 'autobiographical' or 'imaginary'.[69]

Murnane's recounting of this first story addresses both these questions and his own initial question '*Must I write?*' His story was not imaginative in a traditional sense (Murnane has repeatedly insisted that he has no imagination and is not interested in the concept), but rather was inspired by a complex interaction between his reading, his own life, and his recurrent interests. Moreover, Murnane's unusual writing is in a very real sense a *homemade* experimental fiction: his interests and approaches developed early and out of the materials at hand, which were often popular fictions of various kinds. Murnane later enthusiastically read a great deal of literature that forms part of the international avant-garde, but the suggestion from *Barley Patch* is that Murnane's seemingly avant-garde dispositions have much more ordinary sources: his idiosyncratic avant-gardism seems impossible to separate from his own self-identification as a particular kind of bad reader, who had no interest in (and actively avoided) the 'good' reading of institutionalised literary studies.

Even Murnane's preference for long sentences seem reducible, in part, to his paraliterary education rather than avant-garde principles. In his essay, 'In Praise of the Long Sentence', he notes his objection to Frank Kermode's praise of a sentence by Thomas Pynchon, arguing that the 'passage quoted is not a sentence' but rather 'sixty-six words followed by a comma and then a sequence of clauses and phrases that is neither a part of the sentence preceding it nor a sentence in itself'.[70] Murnane contrasts this avant-garde mode of writing with his humbler method: 'I write sentences. I write first one sentence, then another sentence. I write sentence after sentence'.[71] Murnane's description potentially alludes to the narrator's description of his compositional method in Lawrence Sterne's *Tristram Shandy*: 'for I begin with writing the first sentence—and trusting to Almighty God for the second'.[72] Murnane rejects agrammatical prose: 'I never needed to violate the principles of traditional grammar'.[73] This predilection is also opposed to academic criticism, when he registers surprise that a well-known critic like Frank Kermode 'seemed not to know what constituted a sentence'.[74] As to his love of long sentences, Murnane mentions his early reading of older works of fiction by 'R.L. Stevenson, Charles Kingsley, Charles Reade, William Henry Hudson'[75]. Murnane's unusual prose style is thus atavistic as well as avant-garde, drawing on the nineteenth-century writing consumed as part of his paraliterary upbringing, as well as the experimental prose of modernist writing.

Murnane's compositional method reflects these early forms of 'bad' reading. The manor that appears in his childhood story is already characteristically Murnanian, since grand houses recur throughout his fiction, including *Barley Patch*. But what do they signify? Gelder and Salzman's claim that Murnane's work valorises 'pastoral settlement'[76] seems in part based on the frequent appearance of these manors as settings, but the unexpected influence of *The Glass Spear* suggests something entirely different: manor houses are a gothic trope drawn from the popular fiction of Murnane's youth. The narrator of *Barley Patch* remembered the homestead in *The Glass Spear* vividly, because the description was so detailed that a reader could 'draw an accurate plan of the building'.[77] The influence of the gothic on Murnane's fiction, in general, and the large houses in his work, in particular, shouldn't be surprising, given his avowed love for *Wuthering Heights.* Manor houses in Murnane's work function as a 'floating signifier': they have no inherent meaning, but instead constitute a trope that accrues significance through contexts that vary from work to work. Arguably, all of the fixations in Murnane's writing have this floating quality.

Barley Patch offers one personal reason for this recurrent fascination. The narrator notes that even at the age of ten, he had never been inside a two-storey house, and retained an intense 'longing to have access to an upper-storey window'.[78] Here, the manor house is linked with another Murnanian obsession: the window. The two are conjoined as inaccessible objects of childhood fantasy, which is to say as overdetermined fixations, rather than symbols with a clear meaning. This overdetermination becomes generative in Murnane's work because he deploys these obsessive fantasies in subtle variations that produce wildly different literary effects. In *Barley Patch,* the narrator visits his cousins' house, which he mistakenly thinks will have two storeys. Although the house has no second storey, his female cousins do have a two-storey dollhouse. They will not let him play with it and the implication is that—as a boy—his interest in the dollhouse is inappropriate. When everyone has gone to sleep, the narrator surreptitiously peers through the upper windows of the dollhouse, an action that presents the symbolic reverse of the fantasy: instead of looking out from the second story, his perspective is spatially reversed, as a 'giant' looking in.

The dollhouse represents a gendered division between the narrator and his cousins, who do not like him, because he 'begged to see into their doll's house or, failing that, to join in their games or their conversations'.[79] Several other figures in *Barley Patch*, including Aunt Bee from *Brat Farrar* and a nun at his school, are criticised because they rigidly enforce gendered distinctions between children. The narrator himself is so nervous about being discovered later that night that he does not 'insert … through another window one or more finger' to touch the items in the dollhouse lest he 'leave some trace of my intrusion'.[80] This scene is then contrasted with a *Mandrake the Magician* cartoon in which an enormous hand breaks through a glass window to 'grope towards' a woman inside.[81] The combination here is odd and perhaps shocking, since the narrator's timid childhood interest in a dollhouse is compared with a cartoonish act of sexual aggression. Moreover, the language around the initial scene with the dollhouse is oddly sexualised ('I had intended to insert soon afterwards through another window one or more finger …'[82]), which draws together the two scenes, and also echoes the dirty joke in the story 'Finger Web' from *Velvet Waters* about the 'young woman who had been bitten on the funnel by a finger-web spider'.[83] This seemingly innocent childhood memory accrues sexual and voyeuristic connotations.

These implications are confirmed at the end of the novel when the protagonist of the abandoned novel, *O, Dem Golden Slippers*, takes his binoculars to the upstairs window of a friend's flat to spy into the room of a young woman—a literal and disturbing act of voyeurism that is, however, unsuccessful. The link back to the early scenes is specific: the binoculars are described as belonging 'in a bedroom on the upper storey of a doll's house' and the narrator fantasises about the woman 'as a character in a comic strip'.[84] The resonances here are uncomfortable—and intentionally so. The seemingly banal object of childhood fascination—the doll house and its upstairs window—becomes a sexual fetish. This voyeuristic fetish is rearticulated in the chief character's plan to create a 'Black Mass' in a large repurposed church that would involve a sexual orgy; the chief character would never participate, preferring to 'slip unnoticed into the front-pew' and 'masturbate quietly'.[85]

One of the overarching themes of Murnane's work is his rejection of the sexual mores of his Catholic upbringing: the shame of desire, in particular, and the body, in general. Murnane's own files infamously contains a folder that includes 'a detailed account of a mental game devised by Gerald Murnane in the early 1990s in order to indulge his various sexual fantasies'.[86] Sexual desire is treated more or less like other objects in his fiction—and often equated with other types of desire and pleasure, including, most notably, love of landscape. In perhaps the most vivid example of this, Adrian Sherd masturbates in the bathroom of a train while looking out the window:

> With his eye still at the window he reached inside his trousers and took out a part of himself that had always responded to stirring landscapes. He did not even have to think of some girl or woman in his country. A peculiar cluster of vague golden hills, detached from all known continents drifted past him. Before they were gone he had poured out his seed into the toilet bowl.[87]

This scene, much like masturbation at the Black Mass in *Barley Patch,* is meant to be both crude and ridiculous. Murnane's love of 'dirty jokes' is well-known, and these moments can be read as an ironic and proleptic criticism of the apparent voyeurism in Murnane's work—as if Murnane is both acknowledging and dismissing the voyeuristic tendences of his upper-storey observers by pushing it to an intentionally absurd limit.

In the case of *Barley Patch,* the absurdity of the Black Mass is underscored when we discover the real intention behind creating this imaginary house of ill-repute: upstairs the protagonist intends to build surreptitiously a miniature horseracing track. The lurid ceremony below is simply a front for another private, fetishistic obsession in the form of this horseracing game. The connection with the dollhouse is again direct, since the chief character imagines looking at the miniature racecourse 'through a pair of binoculars held back-to-front to his eyes',[88] which would make the miniature horses appear as if they were actual size. But this also underscores the degree to which Murnane casts his own interests in horseracing as a mode of voyeurism. Not only does watching races involve the use of binoculars in a literal sense, but also Murnane has recounted that, while he was discussing his love of racing on an early date with his wife, 'I, the would-be expert on all things equine, was then put in the humiliating position of having to admit that I had never sat astride a horse'.[89] The fetishistic nature of these interests is implicitly acknowledged when the narrator reflects on a photo of Carl Jung that accompanies an article from *Time* magazine in which Jung decided to play 'his favourite childhood games in the hope of learning about himself'.[90]

Jung offers both a justification of Murnane's persistent interest in his childhood obsessions and an ironic acknowledgment of the compulsive nature of these interests.

The obsessive nature of the narrator's interests becomes an insurmountable barrier to answering the question, 'Must I write?' *Barley Patch*—following the logic of Rilke's quotations—returns to Murnane's childhood to understand both why he has written and why he has ceased to write but all he discovers are the various fixations that motivated him to write in the first place, and which continue to animate his fiction. Just as the question 'Must I write?' forms the basis for the writing of *Barley Patch,* so, too, do the investigations of his early sources of authorial inspiration only prompt more writing. The tautological nature of Murnane's investigation is signalled in the title *Barley Patch,* which refers to a neighbour's 'patch of barley' that adjoined the 'tamarisk trees' that were the site of Murnane's childhood racing games as described in his first novel, *Tamarisk Row.*[91] *Barley Patch* is in this sense a sequel to *Tamarisk Row*—but in referring back to his first novel, Murnane reveals the continuity between his old work and new work.

Murnane's late fiction—all of it—derives its power from returning to the questions and ideas that motivated his earlier fiction. One of the most characteristic answers to the question, 'Must I write?' in *Barley Patch* occurs when he discusses the ending of 'The Interior of Gaaldine':

> Nearly sixteen years ago, I stopped writing fiction. A few years later, I wrote a piece of fiction intended to explain why

> I had so stopped. Now, more than ten years later again, I am trying to compose a passage of fiction that might explain my explanatory piece.[92]

Murnane has elsewhere described his writing as forming connections[93] or a 'pattern of meaning'.[94] But the description here suggests that Murnane's late fiction presents a process of re-engaging with the meaning of his earlier writings in ways that also revise and change them. Murnane's earlier work is drawn from the past back into the present, persisting in a ghostly afterlife where the settled meanings of former works are still mutable.

The Author Is Absent: *A History of Books*

A History of Books pushes Gerald Murnane's stylistic mannerisms to their limit. While anaphora has always been a key element of his style, *A History of Books* attains the status of rhetorical ostinato:

> The image-boy-man sometimes looked out through the image-window above his image-desk at an image-view of low green image-hills with a line of image-trees in the image-distance. The image-trees were the nearest image-trees of an image-woodland that extended a little in among the image-hills. The image-boy-man admired the image-trees but had never wished to go alone into the image-woodland.[95]

The prefix 'image-' appears 355 times within the book and demarcates fictional entities that are not to be mistaken for actual ones. The insistent use of 'image-' is both provocative and absurd, parodying realist conventions of verisimilitude: this stylistic choice seems closer to the French *nouveau roman*, than most contemporary Australian novels. As Nicholas Birns has noted, *A History of Books* slyly invokes 'the European avant-garde and an Australian tradition of innovation' through the figure of Christopher Brennan, the Australian poet most closely aligned with the French symbolist movement.[96] Murnane's own avant-garde use of repetition is further intensified through periphrastic self-reference: 'The man mentioned finally began to read the book mentioned in his fortieth year, according to the records that he kept of the books of fiction that he had bought and read'.[97] This sentence is formal and precise (the records include books 'bought' *and* those subsequently 'read'), but its meticulous distinctions are prolix. A more straightforward revision might read: 'According to his records, the man read the book when he was forty'. Such passages will do little to sway Murnane's critics, who see his writing as obsessive and repetitious, but Murnane can write short, clear sentences. The awkward phrasing here constitutes another 'distancing device', separating Murnane's fictionalised autobiography from standard memoir by foregrounding its artificiality.

This slim novella is a ramified memoir. Its title is literal: *A History of Books* is autobiography refracted through Murnane's experiences as a reader, and its twenty-nine unnumbered sections are connected by a formal conceit: each contains a personal reminiscence linked to a specific book. While Murnane is the subject of *A History of Books*, his life appears in fragments—a collage of reminiscences that suggest a larger shape. But at the heart of the novel is a conspicuous absence: none of the recollected books or authors are named. The novella dramatises this absence in the fifth section: a young man sitting in the State Library of Victoria uses a razor blade to remove four black-and-white passport-sized photographs from a large reference volume, entitled *Twentieth Century Authors*. This removal is carried out in secret to avoid the attention of a librarian in a high wooden seat that resembles a 'pulpit' in the middle of the room where he sits watching the readers.[98] In connecting the librarian with a priest and the library with a 'cathedral'[99]—a fairly literal description of the vaulted ceiling of the reading room in the State Library—the young man's actions appear blasphemously iconoclastic. The connection to religious iconography is significant because Murnane often describes religious pictures and cards from his childhood, and the young man here is removing these authors for a similar purpose: he will hang them with tape above the card table that serves as a writing desk in the bungalow where he lives.[100] They are writerly icons for this young writer who resembles the real Gerald Murnane.

My attempt to verify whether the photos of these authors were removed from the book Murnane describes—Stanley Kunitz and Howard Haycroft's *Twentieth Century Authors* (first edition 1942, second edition 1955)—at the State Library of Victoria was initially foiled by its online system. You cannot check-out multiple copies of the same title from the onsite facility where obscure volumes are stored. I approached a librarian explaining that I was a scholar writing a book on Gerald Murnane and needed to physically inspect each copy of this rarely used title. 'Why do you need to see each copy physically?'

the librarian asked. When I explained that I was ascertaining whether or not he might have vandalised these books in the late 1950s or early 1960s, she made a swift chopping motion and said 'Where does this Gerald Murnane live? I will cut off his hand!'

I discovered no incriminating evidence: all remaining volumes in the library are intact. I did, however, locate three of the four images that Murnane discusses. It is lucky that I was able to identify any, since the descriptions are so vague: 'a man with long black hair and a full black beard', 'a man with short blonde hair', 'a man wearing a patch over his left eye', and 'a bald man of middle age'; the fourth author remains unknown because even the narrator cannot recall his name or the details of his photograph.[101] While the man with the eyepatch is readily identifiably as James Joyce, two others (Mikhail Petrovic Artzybashev and Frank Wedekind) are only identifiable because the novella contains a publishers' note at the end which lists the names of the thirty-six authors who are discussed in the book; among those on this list is one 'Gerald Murnane'.[102]

Works of modernist literature often string together famous and obscure quotations from classic works; T.S. Eliot's *The Waste Land* remains the most famous example, and Eliot even included explanatory footnotes in the first book-length edition in the US (Boni & Liveright 1922) to help readers pick the references. Allusions of this kind serve multiple purposes: they signal the intellectual and aesthetic tradition that the work of literature is operating in; they deepen and complexify their own contexts through reference; and they also constitute a highbrow game of *Name That Tune*, as readers try to guess the sources. Murnane's indirect references to writers do not function like traditional allusions because they are virtually impossible to identify. *A History of Books* could be subtitled 'the case of the missing authors'. Following the metaphor of this razor-wielding young man, there is a sense of menace to the way that these authors have been excised from the text, and *A History of Books* is filled with allusions to violence, madness, and suicide. But the omission of these authors' names also constitutes a specific form of literary refusal.

Unlike the infinite deferral of Bartleby's 'I'd prefer not to…' in Herman Melville's short story 'Bartleby, the Scrivener', Murnane's refusal is secretive: he withholds names, references, and crucial contextual information. The narrator of *A History of Books* draws our attention to this when he reveals that the final paragraph of his novel *Inland* is identical to the end of *Wuthering Heights*—though no-one noticed at the time:

> *I lingered round them, under that benign sky; watched the moths fluttering among the heath and hare-bells; listened to the soft wind breathing through the grass; and wondered how anyone could ever imagine unquiet slumbers, for the sleepers in that quiet earth.*[103]

The provenance of *Inland*'s ending was not acknowledged in the book because *Wuthering Heights* was in the public domain. No-one noticed because they couldn't remember 'more than a few words or phrases from the text' as is the case for most readers.[104] *Inland*'s ending quotation is placed in italics, setting it off from the main body of the text, but it does not function like modernist allusion, since few readers would presume that one book would appropriate wholesale the ending of another. Nicholas Birns has argued that critics overlooked the provenance of the ending because they would not associate Murnane's writing with a book like *Wuthering Heights;* this results from a misreading—'the frequent misdiagnosis of Murnane's introversion and subjectivity as solipsism'—in which Murnane's novels are seen as self-referential experiments, rather than works that address emotions and large themes, such as 'tragic love'.[105] But Murnane almost wishes to be misunderstood. He chose not to quote the source and could do so precisely because the original is out of copyright. Here, allusion functions almost like a secret code.

Secrets are important throughout Murnane's fiction. Within the many filing cabinets of his archives, there exists a folder of 'messages written ... to an imaginary future reader', which is entitled '*Titkos dolgok*', a Hungarian phrase meaning 'secret matters'.[106] For Murnane, secret worlds and people have a genuine existence, as in the case of his Ideal Reader. As he told Shannon Burns, these entities 'exist at about three removes from the room in which we're sitting ... through the means of fiction, of writing it and reading it, I've discovered a world that I would never have known otherwise'.[107] Secrets, for Murnane, are linked to flickering, ecstatic visions where the lines between worlds become visible. But Murnane also satirises his own fixation on secrets: in a recent discussion with Merve Emre about Murnane's works, Joseph Steinberg noted that another one of Murnane's files is entitled '*Faszom mertekei stb*', which translates to 'My dick measurements, etc.'; as Steinberg argues 'it's a gesture of concealment' by 'hiding in Hungarian' and 'limiting the reader's access to that information' but it also simultaneously reduces 'to the point of absurdity' the 'aspirations of his fictions' since the secret is both personally revealing, but also hides a childish joke.[108] The ending of *Inland* should be understood in a similar context: the appropriation of the final lines of *Wuthering Heights* is a way of making his own text contiguous with a beloved work of fiction, but also a provocative joke that produces ironic, generative doubling: *Inland* becomes a strange doppelganger of *Wuthering Heights*.

We don't need close reading to understand the importance of omission in Murnane's fiction. He states it explicitly on the first page of *A Million Windows:* 'One of the commonest devices used by writers of fiction is the withholding of essential information'.[109] As Mark Byron has argued, Murnane's style is characterised by 'understatement, lack of disclosure, and missed declarations'.[110] Murnane's literary deployment of secrecy and omission is an example of *apophasis*. In rhetoric, apophasis refers to instances in which evidence is raised only by denial; for example, a candidate in a political debate might say, 'I have no wish today to discuss my opponent's long history of corruption allegations …' as a way of invoking this very history of corruption. Literary forms of apophasis, however, often intersect with the philosophical and theological tradition of approaching truth by the *via negativa,* or what is more commonly called negative theology. Susan Sontag's essay 'The Aesthetics of Silence' describes literary apophasis in these terms, noting that just as 'the activity of the mystic must end in a via negativa, a theology of God's absence, a craving for the cloud of unknowingness beyond knowledge … so art must tend toward anti-art, the elimination of the "subject"... and the pursuit of silence'.[111] This silence recurs in Murnane's fiction, particularly under the guise of monastic vows. The excision of the authors from *A History of Books*—as well as his many other secretive gestures—also exemplifies this 'energetic secular blasphemy'[112] that employs apophatic methods of mysticism to new aesthetic ends. For Sontag, secretive withholding, which she aligns with 'silence' is an exemplary mode of art after modernism, which is 'committed to the idea that the power of art is located in its power to negate'.[113] Christopher Knight—in tracing a modern tradition of literary apophasis from Henry James to Derrida—has argued that 'apophaticism [is] a hitherto unacknowledged conjunct of irony' and constitutes a way of introducing ambiguity into literary discourse while also offsetting the potential corrosive properties of irony.[114]

Apophasis is crucial for understanding *A History of Books:* while, on the one hand, it is an oblique and avant-garde novella, on the other hand, it is arguably one of Murnane's most personal and revealing works—especially in the ways that it details the narrator's relationship with his wife, which appears to be a genuine reflection of aspects of the real-life Murnane's relationship with Catherine, who had died while Murnane was in the process of writing it. Murnane's enduring love for his wife is clear. On the day I visited him, he asked that, on my way out of town, I follow him to one specific and final location: the grave of Catherine and the accompanying plot where he will be buried next to her. Catherine also shared her name with the female protagonist of Murnane's cherished *Wuthering Heights,* and—like that fictional Catherine—her presence haunts

A History of Books. As if to confirm this indirectly, one section contains a ghost story, in which a recently deceased woman appears to have influenced the outcome of a horse race.[115]

The novella opens by referring to a scene of domestic violence that appears to be drawn from Miguel Angel Asturias's 1971 novel *Bejeweled Boy* that, like *A History of Books* is comprised of disjointed narratives (and, although Murnane disliked the novel, it may have influenced his *Landscape with Landscape*, since the earlier sections of Asturias's novel seem to have been dreamed by a young boy who appears in its final section). In the scene described, a man and woman are in a town square and 'once, at least, the woman struck the man and was struck in return'[116] before they unexpectedly transform into animals. This scene from Asturias's novel mirrors an apparently recounted argument between a couple in Melbourne during which 'the woman struck the man and was struck in return'.[117] This opening is both troubling and confusing at the level of sense, because it layers the fictional on top of the actual. Nonetheless, it quickly establishes marital discord—in hostile forms—as one its major themes.

In a key passage, Murnane—then an aspiring author—considers the dramatic personal lives of two writers: Frederick Exley and George Gissing. Gissing married a woman who died as a result of her alcohol addiction and then married another woman who was ultimately 'committed to a so-called infirmary for the insane'.[118] Exley had been repeatedly hospitalised due both to his alcoholism and to other issues related to mental illness. The young Murnane sees his own life as comparatively 'uneventful', and as a result the only possible subject for his future autobiography would be 'the books that he had read'.[119] It might appear that this is what we are now reading: the bookish biography of an author's ordinary life.

Instead, we are told the story of a forty-year-old man who is standing beside his wife in an emergency room; she is strapped to a gurney and screaming that her husband had tried to have her fired from her job and was hospitalising her under false pretences. These paranoid delusions had been occurring for half a decade and would occasionally spill over into violence and abuse when the woman 'had struck him' or when she would call him at work threatening to take an overdose of medicine if he did not come home; she also experienced intense depressive episodes during which she 'kept mostly to her room, sometimes crying out and often smoking cigarettes'.[120] The scene in the hospital is the culmination of these events: after the woman swallowed a large quantity of medicine, the man called an ambulance to have her taken into hospital where he subsequently views her through a 'small window' in a cell with 'upholstered walls and floor'.[121] Here, the Murnanian fixations—the solitary person in a room, the window, and the cell—return in an unexpected and distressing context. Rather than being a bookish biography of an uneventful life, this novella obliquely employs books as a mechanism by which both Murnane and his readers can distantly view traumatic events. This also explains the novel's repeated interest in books that represent madness, including Henry Handel Richardson's *The Fortunes of Richard Mahoney* (1930), which depicts a woman who cares for her 'insane husband' and Elias Canetti's *Auto-da-Fé* (1935), in which a character sends a telegram that reads 'AM COMPLETELY CRACKERS'.[122]

Murnane published his eulogy for his wife, Catherine Murnane, in a 2009 issue of *Scratchpad*, the magazine of the Australia and New Zealand Amateur Publishing Association. It is a moving and loving piece of writing, though characterised by surprising candour: he notes the composure with which she accepted a terminal cancer diagnosis surprised him because she was not 'a calm or patient person' and often 'fretted and complained when things had gone against her'.[123] Murnane also notes that, although she no longer participated in organised religion, she believed 'that a part of her would survive the death and decay of her body. I too believe that and with perhaps even more confidence'.[124] He describes her as 'always a well-dressed lady' who had 'a taste for elegance' despite being from a humble background.[125] We learn that Catherine was not only a dedicated reader (he describes her joy in reading Henry Lawson), but also belatedly became a writer, having 'left behind a manuscript' of 'her autobiography until the age of twenty-five'.[126] The eulogy briefly covers the traumatic material in *A History of Books*, but in a very different light, noting that for 'some years during the 1980s, Catherine suffered from a mental illness'; while they tried to 'keep up the pretense that nothing was wrong' and 'Catherine even dragged herself to work' these were 'tough years' during which the 'family came close to breaking up' before 'Catherine began to recover'.[127] Murnane quotes Robert Musil shortly thereafter noting that 'major events in our lives render us incapable of uttering anything but commonplace sentiments'.[128]

This quotation from Musil may help explain the unusual form that memoir takes in *A History of Books:* its disjointed, bookish, and oblique approach to autobiography constitutes a modernist attempt to defamiliarise 'commonplace sentiments'. *A History of Books* applies fictional techniques to the material of life not to embellish it, but to generate a deeper kind of truth. This process blurs the fictive and the actual, a literary sfumato suggested in the book's final sentence, which seeks the place 'where the land seemed to meet, or even to merge, with the sky, the visible with the invisible'.[129] This is a classically apophatic goal: the desire for truth that evades logic and binaries, and which can be approached only indirectly or negatively.

The blurring of fiction and real life moves in both directions. In one section, he recounts the period of two years during which he negotiated with his wife that she would go to work and he would stay home—doing housework and looking after the children—so that he could write a book 'that he had wanted for many years to write'.[130] Close readers of Murnane's work will recognise this as the same situation of the narrator in the short story 'When the Mice Failed to Arrive' (1989). *A History of Books* reveals a different version of the earlier story: after a few months working on the novel, the writer eventually spends his time 'doing crossword puzzles or having his left hand play against his right hand at Scrabble'; later he begins to 'sip vodka from a flask' which he would hide before his wife returns home.[131] He hides his lack of productivity through an elaborate ruse—typing up pages of another author's work—which is the same trick used by the protagonist of *A Fan's Notes;* at the end of the two years he is only too happy to return to work and leave this state of idle stagnation. While this anecdote serves as a comic and critical appraisal of his past self, it also reveals a surprising autobiographical resonance in one of Murnane's most famous fictional creations: this is exactly the situation of the filmmaker protagonist of *The Plains*, who finds himself unable to finish his film about the Plains, despite having all of the time and resources he might need to complete his project. In such moments of surprising correlation, the idea of Murnane's work as a fundamentally autobiographical project becomes more and more plausible.

If *A History of Books* is autobiographical, the subject of the text—the selfhood of its author—remains fragmented. There is no consistent 'self' portrayed in the novella, though the narrator's various interests and desires do persist over time; As Anthony Uhlmann states, in Murnane's fiction 'there are layers of self that are recounted, and these selves do not all believe the same things'.[132] We are presented snapshots of a self that is dramatically unfolding, but also radically inconsistent as the thoughts and desires of the younger man ironically clash with what the apparent older self—in the form of the narrator and implied author—already knows. This gesture mimics the removal of the author photos that is the central image of *A History of Books*, because the identity of its 'real' author, the living person named Gerald Murnane, remains missing. The radical unknowability of the life of the actual author contrasts drastically with the seemingly coherent personage of the Murnanian narrator. Even as the novella draws on the material of Murnane's real life for its content, it formally acknowledges that the 'real' author—if, indeed, such a thing exists—lives somewhere outside of the text. *A History of Books* reflects Murnane's reluctance to describe his work as autobiography, because autobiography must itself be a fiction, a static depiction of a self that has evolved and changed over time. The novella overcomes this problem formally by depicting different versions of the self over time, while also presenting a kind of fictionalised truth that rises above the commonplaces of everyday life.

A Million Windows and the Implied Author

Gerald Murnane's *A Million Windows* reads like an experimental satire of creative writing instruction: over its 192 pages, the novel openly disparages writing manuals that discuss character, plot, dialogue and other such terms. The narrator can 'hardly believe that anything so foolish was once delivered as advice to intending writers'.[133] He calls plot both 'irrelevant' and 'scarcely comprehensible' as a concept.[134] Dialogue is 'the crudest of the many devices' used by writers.[135] He rejects the idea of meaning, opting instead for a 'connectedness' that corresponds to 'the emergence of a rudimentary pattern' out of the details of the author's life.[136] He despises the notion of character (despite using this word 203 times in the novel), which does not show adequate 'respect' for '*fictional personages*' who have a semiautonomous existence, which means that authors cannot simply direct their actions according to their whim.[137] Rather than using the term 'imagine' or imagination, the narrator prefers to 'speculate about'.[138] As regards point of view, he only writes in first-person and rejects the usage of the 'pretend-narrator,' which is to say narrators who could not be the author because they are 'of a different gender' or 'from a different historical world'.[139] *A Million Windows* is thus a creative writing manual chiefly useful for producing novels in the style of Gerald Murnane.

The novel presents a self-reflexive meditation on writing and reading, but the narrator strongly differentiates his kind of writing from the postmodern practitioners of metafiction—such as John Barth, John Fowles, B.S. Johnson and Robert Coover—and cannot recall 'admiring … self-referential fiction' or 'trying to write' it.[140] He feels 'repelled' by 'extreme examples' in which narrators pretend that they cannot decide between the events that might follow in the narrative.[141] The narrator argues that authors of such novels incorrectly presume fictional characters exist in the same way as real people and can be visually observed like we view characters in a film; instead, the fictional world that characters inhabit is 'vast and vague', 'nowhere to be seen', and therefore entirely unlike reality where readers and authors exist.[142] For Murnane, metafiction fails because it equates two entities—the fictional and the actual—that are incomparable. 'Any writer claiming otherwise,' the narrator states, could never 'be anything but a fool'.[143] Presumably, however, there are *some* metafictional writers that Murnane enjoys, since his enthusiasm for Borges and Italo Calvino is well-known. This critique of self-referential fiction illustrates that Murnane's own self-reflexivity is motivated by practical concerns. The narrator of *A Million Windows* claims his writing 'prevents' readers from experiencing the reality effect of film that falsely equates the actual with fiction. Murnane preserves the otherness of fiction through 'considered narration'—a technique that requires a 'strong narrator' who does not hide behind his 'subject matter as the author of a filmscript', but selects and interprets the content of the fictional work itself.[144] The most important compositional principle in Murnane's work is his thoroughgoing respect for fiction's alterity. This conviction motivates the narrator's dismissal of an unnamed magical realist novel (most probably Miguel Angel Asturias's *Bejeweled Boy*), because its chapters are meant to be narrated by 'a medley of voices' but the author has not created 'a distinctive prose for each supposed speaker'.[145] Metafictional authors fail because they presume that fictional characters are like real people; Asturias's novel fails because it does not give adequate specificity and agency to the various personages occupying the novel, which is thereby reduced to a simple reflection of the authorial ego.

Murnane's unswerving devotion to a series of unusual compositional principles is responsible for the uniqueness of his work, which is methodical rather than 'experimental'. Given *A Million Windows*' focus on authorial technique, it is fitting that the novel takes its title and epigraph from one of the most famous reflections on novelistic method—Henry James's preface to the 1908 New York edition of *The Portrait of a Lady*. This preface—and particularly its central metaphor of the novelist's creative method—prefigures the content and form of Murnane's work:

> The house of fiction has in short not one window, but a million—a number of possible windows not to be reckoned,

> rather; every one of which has been pierced, or is still pierceable, in its vast front, by the need of the individual vision and by the pressure of the individual will.[146]

For James, what the author views through the windows of the house of fiction comprises the novel's subject. The shape of the window—that 'pierced aperture, either broad or balconied or slit-like and low-browed'—constitutes its 'literary form'. The third and most important component of the metaphor, however, is the 'watcher', because form and content are 'as nothing without [this] posted presence'. James elevates the author—a literal elevation since the author looks down through the window to the subject matter below—because authorial disposition dominates the text: 'Tell me what the artist is,' James asserts, 'and I will tell you of what he has been conscious'[147]. It is precisely this relation between authorial consciousness and fiction that *A Million Windows* critically scrutinises. *A Million Windows* initially seems Jamesian, because the novel's various narratives, digressions and remembrances cohere through the singular voice of the narrator, who gives shape and form to these fragments of experience. Meaning agglomerates slowly as events, memories and allusions are connected in unexpected ways. Readers are given access to private details of the author's life, which generates both intimacy and claustrophobia. Much of *A Million Windows*, like Murnane's other fiction, operates in a confessional mode: the narrator describes his problems with drinking, aspects of his troubled upbringing, mental illness, two encounters that appear to have been extramarital affairs, and other deeply personal and traumatic experiences.

A Million Windows appropriates James's conception of 'The House of Fiction' in the most literal way possible: the narrator resides with many other authors in one wing of an enormous mansion that he refers to as the 'House of Fiction', where they write, share stories, reflect on novelistic methods and partake in elaborate rituals based on James' writing. Here, the 'House of Fiction' is transformed into a characteristically Murnanian setting. I have already noted Murnane's love of large manor houses, which appears to stem from his childhood reading of gothic fiction. But the House of Fiction draws on another setting that recurs throughout Murnane's writing: the monastery. The Cistercian monastery at Yarra Glen comprises a key setting in Murnane's early novel, *A Season on Earth,* which has recurred throughout his work. The manor in *The Plains* becomes a secular monastery in which the unnamed filmmaker devotes his life to the aesthetic contemplation of *The Plains.* Another secular monastery is the Waldo writers retreat in 'Stone Quarry' where writers undertake a vow of silence that resembles the 'Great Silence' of the Cistercian monks in *A Season on Earth.*[148] In *Border Districts,* the narrator discusses another writers' retreat, which he imagines as including 'cabins' arranged like 'the cells were arranged in a certain community of monks' of 'the Carthusian order'.[149] The House of Fiction—though the narrator later admits it does not actually exist—is yet another aesthetic commune.

A Million Windows may appropriate James's metaphor, but it also undermines it from the opening sentence: 'The single holland blind in his room was still drawn down in late afternoon'.[150] The mere appearance of this single holland blind revises James's metaphor, because there is neither window nor view, only the solitary consciousness of the author at work. This imaginary writer is closed off from the outside world, but his inner world extends in two fictional dimensions: he is a character inside Murnane's work of fiction but is also writing his own work, which the reader encounters in one solitary sentence. But the sentence he writes is not his own creation; instead it is a 'remembered version of a quotation … he had read long before'[151]; the subject matter of his fiction is not reality but other books. Following this logic, the million windows of Murnane's title might be best conceived of not as the proliferating external windows of an endless house, but as an infinite regress of nested windows opening into inner worlds rich in exquisite detail. Appropriately, the narrator notes that the narrative dimension of fiction can be seen 'extending infinitely sideways in opposite directions'.[152]

The sentence written by this imaginary author is 'All our troubles arise from our being unwilling to keep to our room'.[153] This is a gloss on a line from Pascal's *Pensées*: 'j'ai souvent dit, que tout le malheur des hommes vient de ne savoir pas se tenir en repos dans une chambre',[154] though the source is characteristically withheld. Even without knowing the provenance of this quotation, it will evoke Murnane's frequent references to solitary writers, often seated near windows. In *Landscape with Landscape* (1985), the narrator imagines the nineteenth-century Italian writer Giacomo Leopardi 'imprisoned in his parents house' and 'sitting at his desk in deep shadow but in sight of a distant rectangle of white sunlight that was all he saw all day of some far-ranging view of Italian hills'.[155] In *Velvet Waters*,

Murnane provides a catalogue of 'writers whose way of life was more or less solitary', including 'Kafka, Emily Dickinson, Giacomo Leopardi, Edwin Arlington Robinson, Michel de Ghelderode, A.E. Housman, Thomas Merton, Gerald Basil Edwards, C.W. Killeaton'.[156] This last author is the protagonist of Murnane's first novel, *Tamarisk Row*.

Giorgio Agamben has argued that the 'particular power of quotations arises … not from their ability to transmit that past and allow the reader to relive it but, on the contrary, from their capacity to "make a clean sweep, to expel from the context, to destroy"'.[157] Here, Murnane's quotation from Pascal invokes a series of Murnanian associations. It might recall Proust (an author frequently cited by Murnane) in his cork-lined room, or the aphorism of another of Murnane's favourite authors, Franz Kafka:

> You do not need to leave your room. Remain sitting at your table and listen. Do not even listen, simply wait, be quiet, still and solitary. The world will freely offer itself to you to be unmasked, it has no choice, it will roll in ecstasy at your feet.[158]

What appears to be external reference is actually a complex mode of internal reference. This occurs repeatedly in *A Million Windows,* such as when Murnane compares James's metaphor with another metaphor from a biography in which 'distant windows are likened to spots of golden oil'; the reference here is to Hal Porter's *The Watcher on the Cast Iron Balcony,* which describes 'a sunset behind Kensington ridge' that is 'reflected in sumless distant windows like spots of golden oil'.[159]

A Million Windows obsessively returns to questions about the relationship between fiction and the world, between subject matter and literary form, and between readers and authors. It reflects on these matters at greater length than any of Murnane's previous works, though they are hardly new considerations. Murnane revises ideas articulated earlier in his essay 'The Breathing Author' (originally entitled 'I Have Never Worn Sunglasses'), which he first delivered at a conference on his work held in 2001 at the University of Newcastle—a regional university a few hours north of Sydney on the coast of New South Wales. In both texts, Murnane develops a notion derived from the work of the literary critic and rhetorician Wayne C. Booth, called the 'implied author', which Murnane contrasts with 'the breathing author'. Murnane first mentions Booth and this concept in 1995 in the story 'In Far Fields' from *Emerald Blue.* He notes that 'I learned the term *implied author* from the book *The Rhetoric of Fiction* by Wayne C. Booth,' and that by using the term, 'I seemed to be explaining to my students what took place in my mind while I wrote'; the narrator immediately appropriates this concept, arguing that the 'writer of these words' who is the 'I' within the fiction 'is mostly aptly denoted by the words *the implied author of this piece of fiction*'.[160] *A Million Windows* develops this concept of the implied author further:

> The reader should think of me as a *personage* as being in some respects less than an actual person and in other

> respects more so. At the very least, I am a voice: the voice behind the text … or, rather, the *implied* author, by which I mean the personage of whom nothing is known except what can be inferred from this text.[161]

The implied author, for Murnane, is a fictional creation who seems to be real, but is actually a purely textual entity. From this perspective, Murnane's own 'gullible' and paraliterary interests in fictional characters are not strange obsessions, but the logical product of these fictional representations of the author that all novels generate.

Murnane's repeated invocation of Booth is fascinating, given Murnane's generally hostile disposition towards literary criticism. Even in *A Million Windows,* Murnane praises *The Rhetoric of Fiction* (though it is not directly named), but criticises another unnamed scholarly work of narratology—which appears to be Franz K. Stanzel's *A Theory of Narrative* (1984)—that he finds confusing and 'intimidating', despite its inclusion of diagrams that illustrate 'kinds of fictional narration'.[162] Murnane states that, for him, the most useful section of *The Rhetoric of Fiction* for him was the afterword, which contained charts on 'the variety of authors' and the 'variety of readers' most of whom 'exist in the heads' of either writers who are writing or readers who are reading.[163]

As Tom Kindt and Hans-Harald Müller have argued, Booth created the implied author to solve logical problems generated by the 'New Criticism',[164] a school of formalist literary criticism that arose in the mid-twentieth century in the USA and took its name from John Crowe Ransom's book

The New Criticism (1941). Specifically, Booth wanted to avoid running afoul of the 'intentional fallacy' under which any alleged authorial intention that could not be derived through close reading had to be discarded.[165] Booth created the implied author to model the relationship between author and reader within the text in a way that could be analysed by close reading. As Booth states, 'The "views of man" of Faulkner and E.M. Forster ... are only of peripheral value to me as I read their novels. But the implied author of each novel is someone with whose beliefs on all subjects I must largely agree if I am to enjoy his work'.[166] The implied author is thus the author's 'second self',[167] who may interrupt the narrative, appear as a character, be largely identified with the narrator, or else be entirely distant from all of those. The sole goal of the implied author is 'the intuitive apprehension of a completed artistic whole' by a novel's implied reader, the fictional and internal second-self of the reader.[168] For Booth, the implied author determines the aesthetic unity of a literary work, but has no direct relationship to the actual author. Subsequent critics, such as Kindt and Müller, have argued that the creation of the 'implied author' in many ways raises more questions than it answers.[169]

Murnane also references Booth's concept of the 'Flesh-and-Blood-Author', which Murnane prefers to call the 'breathing author'. This is the unknowable and very real author that shadows the 'implied author' we meet in the text. The gap between them may seem miniscule, but for Murnane it is unbreachable. While this may appear to be another distancing device, Murnane's claim here is genuine: it acknowledges that all autobiographical writing, done well, is also necessarily fiction, and that the literary representation of a life, no matter how seemingly accurate, can never be the same as the material experience of living that life. One can also see Murnane's attraction to the idea of authors constructing imaginary readers (we know of Murnane's Ideal Reader) and readers constructing imaginary authors. Moreover, we have already seen that Murnane's fiction often ramifies and fragments the self rather than reaffirming it as a unified whole: the implied author, unlike the self, is consistent and unified.

But Murnane's usage of the term 'implied author' diverges from Booth's in one crucial way. For both Murnane and Booth, the implied author presents a way of understanding how textual intention can be discussed in relation to authors and readers. For both, knowledge of literary works is always textual (about the words), rather than contextual (about the real people who wrote the words). The internal contradictions inherent to Booth's concept, however, are playfully augmented in Murnane's work. What are we to make of the fact that the notion of the implied author in Murnane's work is discussed by the implied author himself? Does this undermine the claim, since it does not belong to the 'real' author? Are there multiple implied authors across Murnane's fiction or are they all the same? Does it matter that these implied authors resemble each other and repeat similar ideas? Is there a difference between the implied authors of Murnane's fictional works and those in his non-fictional works, especially given the claim in *Invisible Yet Enduring Lilacs* that he has never 'tried to write fiction or non-fiction or anything in-between' and should have published 'all my pieces of writing as essays'?[170] Or is this the claim of yet another implied author?

These are unanswerable questions, and it remains unclear how seriously we should take them. The crucial difference between Murnane's and Booth's usage of the implied author is that Murnane delights in the paradoxes generated by the idea, and he exploits them for aesthetically generative ends. As Ivor Indyk states, Murnane's use of the implied author 'creates ironic elaborations on a scale Booth could never have dreamed of'.[171] In 'The Interior of Gaaldine' (1995), the narrator, who resembles Murnane, is given files describing a complex, imaginary horseracing game set in a fictitious country called New Arcadia, which resembles Murnane's Antipodean Archive. Upon reading the files, the narrator notes that:

> The implied author of the pages ... had written the pages in order to cause to arise in the mind of one or another reader of the pages one or another image of a personage who would seem to the reader more likeable and more trustworthy than any person in the place where the reader was reading.[172]

Murnane's claims here draw directly on Booth's, who in a section entitled 'The Implied Author as Friend and Guide', argues that the implied author of Jane Austen in *Emma* is 'a perfect human being, within the concept of perfection established by the book she writes' and that her perfection is of a kind 'not quite attainable in real life'.[173] But Murnane turns this concept of the 'perfect' implied author into a metafictional tautology: the intentional product of Murnane's perfect implied author is the creation of the perfect implied author. But this situation is even more convoluted, since the implied recipient or reader of the text in the story is also the implied author of the text we are reading, and *both* are, in some form, fictional personages who resemble, at least in part, the real Gerald Murnane. Murnane has said that the author of the files is someone 'who devotes his life to an enterprise such as my Antipodean Archive would have become if I had devoted *my* life to it'.[174] The implied author in Murnane's work is not a solution to problems generated by the New Criticism (as for Booth), but is rather a means to create nested fictional ontologies that are then elided in paradoxical formations.

The difference between the implied author and the breathing author nonetheless remains crucial for understanding how Murnane differs from James. As Suzie Gibson has argued, while Murnane 'conjures James' meticulous style', he does not seek to render identifiable characters whose personalities are revealed through 'their past lives, their perceptions of other characters, or, particularly, in conversation'; from this perspective James and Murnane are both prosaic technicians, but that is where their resemblance ends.[175] For James, the work of art cannot be separated from the consciousness of the author (even if it is mediated by literary form and subject matter); for Murnane, the author is always remote and inaccessible, and the work of fiction is not the prismatic sublimation of the writerly ego. Any trace of authorial consciousness—or the 'breathing author', to use Murnane's term—is no more than the attenuated glow of sunlight at the edges of a drawn curtain. Whereas James is certain that he can intuit who the author is based on authorial consciousness, *A Million Windows* rejects this idea at the end of the novel when the narrator, standing on the ground, looks back up at the window of the writer described at the beginning from the opposite perspective: 'I looked up and saw … a window and behind it a drawn blind. In short, I learned nothing'.[176]

The real author is completely inaccessible. James would seem to become a useful foil—a negative example who is too close for comfort. Murnane appears to follow Booth's *Rhetoric of Fiction,* which contains a long section on James's fiction and the use of unreliable narration. Murnane briefly argues 'in favour of reliable narrators' over unreliable ones that are 'discoverable from internal evidence' because the text offers proof that they are 'inconsistent or self-contradictory'.[177] This definition is similar to Booth's, who calls 'a narrator reliable when he speaks for or acts in accordance with the norms of the work (which is to say, the implied author's norms), unreliable when he does not'.[178] But Murnane turns away from this Boothian depiction of James as an author who only uses unreliable narration.

Murnane distinguishes between the person of Henry James and his authorial second-self, noting his lack of 'affinity for the man of flesh and blood' known as Henry James, and his simultaneous feeling of 'comradeship' for the 'personage' who wrote his fiction, which is to say the implied author of James' fiction.[179] He then goes on to quote the preface to *The Golden Bowl,* where James notes his 'preference … for "seeing my story," through the opportunity and the sensibility of some more or less detached … intelligent, witness or reporter, some person who contributes to the case mainly a certain amount of criticism and interpretation of it'.[180] This approach is precisely the kind of implied author and narrator (who, for Murnane, unlike Booth, are always one and the same) that Murnane calls the 'strong narrator'.[181] The strong narrator does not 'hide behind subject-matter', but instead becomes 'the sole interpreter' of it; a strong narrator produces what Murnane terms 'true fiction', a kind of writing that is not real, but also does not pretend to be real because it has its own reality, its own immanent truth.[182] This hybrid form of 'true' fiction seems to be the goal of Murnane's writing.

But one of the qualities of Murnane's fiction is that it resists settled formulas—including the ones that Murnane, or his implied authors, generate. After developing this notion of 'true fiction', the novel complicates this again when the narrator of *A Million Windows* is visited by a 'man from a far northern state' who has papers showing that he and the narrator are half-brothers who share a mother.[183] The half-brother was born a year before the narrator and given up for adoption immediately; in his one attempt to contact his birth mother, she had a solicitor write back to him, threatening legal action—a threat that resulted in the half-brother having a nervous breakdown. The narrator was unaware of all of this information, and cannot explain his mother's actions. After speaking with his aunt, however, the narrator discovers that his mother had been sexually assaulted by her stepfather. This emotionally intense narrative is delivered in a typically detached way, but it is an absolutely shocking ending to a novel that seemed, up to this point, to be an often-theoretical reflection on narrative. It is an excellent example of how Murnane's narratives often obliquely deal with intensely traumatic material, such as sexual assault and incest.

This eruption of real trauma alongside the reflections on method in *A Million Windows* produces an irreconcilable disjuncture, and the narrator himself is open about his inability to imagine what his mother experienced. But the narrator also notes a surprising fictional shadow within his own work: the location where the assault took place, a forest near where he grew up, is one that has previously appeared in Murnane's fiction, and which he had—for no reason that he could understand—remained 'troubled by' even late in his life.[184] He recalls one particular childhood experience in the forest in which his hands had been cut by foliage in the forest and a moment when a brightly-coloured bird, a 'sacred kingfisher', had flown through the sunlight.[185] As Brendan Casey has argued, this scene is itself linked to a scene of bird-trapping in *Wuthering Heights,* which Murnane states has always 'haunted' him.[186] These images and their connection to the forest are evidence that feelings 'emanate from certain image-objects', but this also suggests that the relationship between actual truth and its fictional forms cannot be separated in the way that our narrator wishes to cut off the breathing author from the implied author.

Elsewhere, the narrator notes that 'the details of what we call our lives go sometimes to form patterns of meaning' much like those in fiction.[187] In what appears to be a clear example of life imitating art, the secret divulged at the climax of *A Million Windows* reveals an obscured pattern of meaning that retrospectively unites aspects of his fiction; this pattern, however, can only be uncovered through the process of writing and its accrual of connections. *A Million Windows* does not simply call into question—as so many have done before—the possibility of excavating authorial intention from a text. It suggests that authorial intention is created through the writing and production of the text itself. More importantly, as the novel's revision of material from Murnane's earlier novels suggests, intention may be generated retrospectively, as ideas, characters and scenes are placed in new contexts that enable them to derive entirely new meanings. If *A Million Windows* is, as it appears to be, a late reflection on the artist's own method, it is also an acknowledgment of the necessarily contingent nature of that method, the products of which can often be a surprise, even to their own author.

The Text Ends at This Point: *Border Districts*

Gerald Murnane wrote *Border Districts* intending it to be his last novel, though, as we have seen, he has written multiple 'last books'. *Border Districts* has been Murnane's most decorated novel: it won the Prime Minister's Literary Award for Fiction, and was shortlisted for the Miles Franklin Award, the ALS Gold Medal, and the Christina Stead Prize for Fiction. It was the only one of his novels published after Mark Binelli's *New York Times Magazine* profile, and perhaps Australian prizes could no longer overlook Murnane. It may also be that the composition of awards panels has changed to include judges more sympathetic to his work. Regardless, Murnane is modest about *Border Districts*, calling it a much simpler work than the novels that preceded it, and registering his surprise that it was the one to win, finally, a major Australian award for fiction.

Border Districts—like *Barley Patch*—is motivated by a rhetorical inquiry, as the narrator attempts to explain 'how he came by' an 'odd expression': 'I resolved to guard my eyes'.[188]

The explanation arrives 141 pages later, near the end of the book. The narrator came across the phrase because he was curious about a specific priest and wanted to know the content of his internal thoughts while praying. To this end, he inspects a holy card that was often the object of the priest's attention during prayer. The card reads, '*Guard eyes while in town*'.[189] The narrator imagines that the priest adopted this credo to shield himself from prurient thoughts at 'the sight of image after image of young women with bare legs and low necklines outside the cinemas that he passed'.[190] The narrator supposes that this is motivated by his desire to 'remain true to the image lying between the pages of the book', which depicts the Virgin Mary.[191]

The narrator would be sympathetic to these desires, given that he, also, has recently relocated to the border districts so that he could be 'alone' and live by 'several rules' that he had 'long wanted to live by'.[192] This is unsurprising since monastic living and Marist figures pervade Murnane's fiction. But as Carmel Bird has noted, *Border Districts* particularly foregrounds aspects of religious life—'images of churches, the presence of churchmen, church doctrine'—to remind 'the reader that this narrative is a type of spiritual quest'.[193] The narrator also guards his eyes, but what he avoids looking at directly is a church in town. This fictional detail is grounded in reality: in a short piece on Murnane for *The Paris Review*, Will Heyward notes that Murnane 'stopped near a church off to the right, not far from the road, and soon it became clear that he could not turn to look at it—could not allow himself to see the church, at least not more than peripherally'.[194] While the narrator of

Border Districts might be extremely similar to Murnane, they are not identical, and the novel plays with these slippages between the author's real identity and his fictional manifestations. For example, the narrator's move to a small town in regional Victoria seems to refer to Murnane's own real-life move to Goroke. But the narrator's reasons for moving are different from those of the actual Gerald Murnane, who, as noted earlier, was motivated by familial concerns.

The move to the border districts undertaken both by Murnane and his implied author, recalls the travels of another significant Murnanian narrator, the protagonist of *The Plains*:

> Twenty years ago, when I first arrived on the plains, I kept my eyes open. I looked for anything in the landscape that seemed to hint at some elaborate meaning behind appearances.[195]

Murnane's move to Goroke echoes this fictional move in an inverted form of mimesis. *Border Districts* makes its connection to *The Plains* explicit in its opening lines: 'Two months ago, when I first arrived in this township just short of the border, I resolved to guard my eyes...'[196] This narrator arrived only two months ago, whereas the narrator of *The Plains* is looking back over twenty years. The narrator of *The Plains* has his eyes open, while the narrator of *Border Districts* keeps his eyes guarded. The opposed approaches to vision in the two novels signal the way in which the works are placed in dialogue with each other.

In a 'one-minute lecture' on *The Plains* delivered in 1988 at La Trobe University, a suburban university in northern

Melbourne near where Murnane grew up, he described the novel as 'the story of a man who tried to see properly'.[197] *Border Districts* takes up the question of seeing: the wide-eyed openness of *The Plains*' youthful and naïve narrator is contrasted with this older narrator who has turned inward. In guarding his eyes, the narrator of *Border Districts* does not reject vision as a source of meaning, but instead prefers an indirect, apophatic mode of observation: he guards his eyes to 'be more alert to what appears at the edges of my range of vision' and notice details that seem to 'quiver or be agitated until I have the illusion that I am being signalled or winked at'.[198] The seemingly stoic gesture of guarding one's eyes actually enables a heightened perception that makes the narrator alive to urgent truths and produces ecstatic visions that can only be accessed by foregoing obvious visual pleasures. Their pleasurable nature is underscored by the sexual overtones of the language ('quivering', 'winked'). Moreover, the narrator's decision to 'guard his eyes' ultimately ends in the illusion of being 'winked at', another physical means of guarding one's eye; guarded vision produces the ecstatic vision of a guarded eye. Occluded eyes recur throughout *Border Districts*, as in the case of the 'young woman holding a glass marble firmly between upper and lower eyelid at the front of a normal eye', or the narrator who looks 'down the tube' of a kaleidoscope 'into the afternoon sunlight'.[199]

Despite their different methods, the narrators of *Border Districts* and *The Plains* are both searching for glimpses of a hidden reality: the narrator of *The Plains* looks for things that might 'hint at some elaborate meaning behind appearances'.[200] In both works, vision offers access to sublime encounters that transcend everyday reality. When describing his proposed film, entitled *The Interior*, the narrator of *The Plains* states that 'the hero of my film' will see, 'at the furthest limits of his awareness, unexplored plains'.[201] The notion of truth hidden at the 'limits of awareness' here seems very close to the ideas of the narrator in *Border Districts*. Multiple characters in *The Plains*—including various landowners and several aspiring artists seeking patronage—articulate rival notions of vision and its relationship to meaning.

Perhaps the most significant discussions of vision occur between the unnamed protagonist and his patron. In their first meeting, the patron criticises the idea that the filmmaker might create a 'visible equivalent of the plains' before noting that he 'believed, nevertheless, that I might one day be capable of seeing what was worth seeing'.[202] Here, the narrator's attempt to view the hidden meanings of the plains directly is derided and explicitly attacked as a 'blind' search.[203] The young filmmaker's desire to 'keep his eyes open' is subtly mocked by the description of another patron lying on a 'stretcher' with 'his eyes covered', who 'had not once met my own eyes'.[204] This contrast between the open-eyed narrator and the patron with his eyes covered establishes a dichotomy in the novel between the sensible empirical world and an internal world of mentally generated imagery. This dichotomy is rearticulated in one of the most famous passages of *The Plains*—a long soliloquy from the filmmaker's patron:

> Look. My eyes are closed. I am about to sleep. When you see me insensible, trepan me. Carve my skull neatly open …

> Peer into the pale brain you find pulsating there. Prise apart its dull-coloured lobes. Examine them with powerful lenses. You'll see nothing to suggest plains. They disappeared long ago—the lands I claimed to see.
>
> The Great Darkness. Isn't that where all our plains lie? … We're travelling somewhere in a world the shape of an eye. And we still haven't seen what other countries that eye looks out on.[205]

Some commentators have viewed this passage as a reflection on phenomenology, in which the contours of the sensible world are generated by the processes of perception.[206] Murnane himself has rejected these philosophical readings, but it is notable that the passage engages directly with the issue of vision and representation. Earlier, the patron seemed to argue that the Plains could only be understood through internal mental imagery, but here he completely rejects material explanations of psychology, since the link between mental processes and the physical biology of the brain cannot be scientifically reconstructed in the 'dull-coloured lobes' of the 'pale brain'. For him, the Plains are a realm of 'great darkness' and thus beyond vision or imagination. He reimagines the world as a giant eye that looks out onto other still unseen worlds. This creates an infinite regress of observation: one searches for the hidden essence of the world, only to discover the world itself is observing other still more secret realms. As Nicholas Birns argues, these moments in Murnane's work are 'not seeking merely to divert or to elevate his reader from the material world, but to recognise its immanent fissures and contradictions'.[207]

The point here is not simply that reality, for Murnane, is ineffable, but rather that the layered complexity of reality cannot be adequately captured by rational conceptualisation. This is a characteristically apophatic assertion.

These dialogical arguments about vision culminate in the final scene of *The Plains*, when the narrator attempts to photograph his own eye:

> I lifted my own camera to my face and stood with my eye pressed against the lens and my finger poised as if to expose to the film in its dark chamber the darkness that was the only visible sign of whatever I saw beyond myself.[208]

Paradoxes proliferate in this final sentence: the darkness of the film captures the darkness within the eye—an absence that is also the only material trace of the narrator's vision. It may be tempting to read this passage, following Ihab Hassan, as the merging of 'the observer and observed,'[209] but this interpretation seems to miss the irony and playfulness of the passage. The actual photo produced is taken by the patron, who 'record[s] the moment' by taking a photo of the narrator taking a photo of his own eye. Moreover, this photograph is a parodic response to the patron's other photographs, which depict the filmmaker 'as a man with my eyes fixed on something that mattered'.[210] The final image, in short, is a solipsistic joke. The narrator's original desire to find the 'elaborate meaning behind appearances' has been replaced by a cynical acknowledgment of the inescapable subjectivity of both vision and meaning. The narrator has finally been convinced that the attempt to offer a visual representation of *The Plains* is futile, and his film will never be made. The closest we will get to *The Interior* is the black image of the protagonist's eye.

Border Districts' imperative to guard one's eyes directly replies to this final image in *The Plains.* The narrator of *Border Districts* even states he 'could never bear to have a glass marble, or any other object, resting against the surface of my eye'[211]; Murnane shares this aversion so intensely that he has never worn sunglasses, unlike the protagonist of *The Plains* who stands with his 'eye pressed against the lens' of a camera.[212] Where the end of *The Plains* repeatedly discusses the 'darkness' of the eye and internal mental spaces, *Border Districts* opens by focusing on a 'white patch … against a black ground at the edge of my mind' that will not be 'dislodged', which is the 'white bib' or '*rabat*' of the priest who inspires the narrator to guard his eyes.[213] At the end of the novel, the narrator comes across a photo of the now greatly aged priest still wearing his white robe. He then recalls the image of a stained glass window—which may be a window of the church in town that the narrator prefers not to look at—which shows men 'wearing a robe of black with a white bib' all of whom look out 'from the sides of [their] eyes'.[214] This image brings together, once again, the memory of the priest's white rabat with notion of oblique vision. The final paragraph of *Border Districts* ends with a quotation from Shelley's elegy for Keats, 'Adonais' (despite the fact that the narrator finds the poetry of both Shelley and Lord Byron to be 'fatuous and affected'): 'Life, like a dome of many-coloured glass/Stains the white radiance of eternity'.[215] For me, and perhaps for many others, the immediate association with this poem is Mick Jagger's reading of it in Hyde Park in 1969 as a eulogy for his deceased Rolling Stones bandmate, Brian Jones. Its appearance is surprising, but it is a characteristically Murnanian gesture to take such a well-known quotation and reappropriate it within the context of his fixations.

This final image implies that the monastic desire for purity aspired to by both the priest and the narrator is ultimately unattainable, since life will always stain the 'white radiance of eternity'. Crucially, Murnane also withholds the next line of the Adonais ('Until death tramples it to fragments'), which makes the quotation appear far more positive than it does within the poem; Anthony Uhlmann has argued that, in many ways, the meaning of Shelley's poem is the 'opposite' of Murnane's meaning at the end of *Border Districts*.[216] This matters because the decision to conclude on the 'white radiance of eternity' so clearly counterpoises the 'darkness' in the final sentence of *The Plains*. The two novels present complementary but irreconcilable accounts of reality. *The Plains* relates the experiences of a young man whose idealised notions of *The Plains* give way to a nihilism that imprisons him in his own consciousness. *Border Districts* re-affirms idealism by suggesting that indirect vision can provide transcendent experiences, even if purity itself remains fundamentally unattainable. *The Plains* itself already internally presents dichotomous understandings of reality through its discussion of the rival Horizonites and the Haresman—two groups of plainsmen who develop different approaches to understanding the Plains. As Helen Daniel has argued, the Horizonites focus on the distant vistas offered by the Plains, while the Haresman closely inspect the detail of the

Plains' grasses; their differences are literally perspectival, reflecting 'a tension between the immanent and microscopic' and the 'vast macroscopic world running ineffably far to the horizon'.[217]

Border Districts and *The Plains* are similarly intended to be read as complementary texts: they constitute a novelistic diptych. *The Plains* was originally part of a longer novel entitled *The Only Adam*. The sections about the Plains bookended a longer narrative in the middle, standing 'in relation to the setting of the rest of the book as a mirage stands in relationship to the landscape that gives rise to it'.[218] In other words, *The Plains* was originally meant to exist in a discursive relationship with another, longer (and still unpublished) narrative. Murnane has stated that, for him, these unpublished versions are as real as the published ones: while most readers and critics might think of *The Plains* as a 'text of about 35,000 words', Murnane thinks of it 'as having the title that I first gave it', which was '*Landscape with Darkness and Mirage*' or else he thinks of 'the unpublished work of fiction *The Only Adam*, of which the text of *The Plains* was once part'.[219] Murnane's focus on other versions of *The Plains* reflects his interests in the various alternate versions of himself that appear as 'implied authors' across his works. But this passage also clarifies the relationship of *Border Districts* to *The Plains*. Much in the way that *Barley Patch* repurposed the abandoned text of *O, Dem Golden Slippers*, *Border Districts* re-enacts the original intention of *The Plains*, by once again making it part of a textual diptych. *Border Districts*, from this perspective, becomes a late rewriting of *The Only Adam*. To be clear, based on the small sample of *The Only Adam* that I have heard (Shannon Burns read out a passage at the Goroke

Conference, in which the narrator discusses his love for Spike Milligan's comedy radio programme, *The Goon Show*), *Border Districts* does not necessarily share any direct content with the earlier unpublished novel. However, both *Border Districts* and the other section of *The Only Adam* discursively respond to the 'darkness' and the 'mirage' of *The Plains.*

A key effect of this is that *Border Districts* changes the meaning of *The Plains* proleptically. *The Plains* has been viewed as a standalone novel for the three decades since its publication, rather than as half of a novelistic dyad. Moreover, what had previously appeared to be a definitive conclusion to *The Plains* now becomes an unfolding moment in a larger dialogic structure that occurs across two works. This belated authorial intervention is not accidental, but rather constitutes a process in Murnane's writing, which I am calling 'retrospective intention'. Retrospective intention might best be understood as a process similar to what Borges described as the way in which strong writers effectively generate their own precursors: 'The fact is that every writer creates his own precursors. His work modifies our conception of the past, as it will modify the future'.[220] Borges points out that only after Kafka may we describe earlier writers as being Kafkaesque. Kafka's strong authorial intervention effectively brings into being a new alignment of literary tradition that only becomes apparent after the fact. Borges's influence on Murnane, particularly in stories like 'Land Deal', is clear, and Murnane lists Borges as one of the eight authors whose 'books I would like to read yet again during the years left to me'.[221] Like Borges's concept of literary precursors, Murnane's late writing similarly works in two temporal directions, adding to his body of work while also intentionally altering our perceptions of his past oeuvre.

Through retrospective intention, Murnane is able to impose a seeming coherence that enables his disparate body of work to constitute an aesthetic totality. This totality is essentially fictitious: Murnane has repeatedly disputed any notion that his works constitute a predesigned and coherent aesthetic program. He has often given concrete examples of the failures and discontinuities between his authorial intent and the eventual publication (or not) of his works, including the unpublished *The Only Adam*, the incomplete *O, Dem Golden Slippers*, and the originally much-longer manuscripts of *Tamarisk Row* and *Lifetime on Clouds*. Murnane has repeatedly emphasised that his authorial intention has only had a tenuous link to publication, and that he was often 'ready to accept that what I was writing would never be published' even after he had already published several novels.[222]

In foregrounding the contingency of his published output, any claim for the coherence of Murnane's oeuvre seems foolhardy. But something strange happens in Murnane's late writing, as exemplified by his final novel *Border Districts:* Murnane's late works turn contingency into necessity by reframing and recontextualising this work in such a way that gives it coherence. This actually constitutes a more impressive project than the enactment of an original authorial plan, since it unifies a body of works after the fact through a process of creative intervention. The retrospective coherence of the oeuvre—much like the concept of the implied author—is a textually generated coherence ontologically distinct from the 'real' and contingent history of Murnane's publications. Brendan Casey has noted a similar tendency in Murnane's work and linked it explicitly to Proust's notion of 'retrospective illumination' in which the unity of a work of art is only discovered through the process of writing, after the fact.[223] Retrospective intention demonstrates the capacity of the fictional to overcome the contingencies of reality. Murnane's legacy becomes one not of following an established plan of authorial development, but rather of being able to generate the sense of one, where no such thing existed. *Border Districts* enacts a retrospective revision of intention that is both textual and fictitious, but nonetheless functions as a material corrective to the contingencies of publishing by returning *The Plains* to something like the discursive relationship envisioned in its original conception. Here, intention simultaneously becomes original, delayed, and retrospective all at once, and one of the key virtues of fiction in Murnane's writing is precisely that it can transcend these limitations of the material world.

Conclusion: Gerald Murnane's Late Style

Gerald Murnane's final four novels are exemplary works of 'late style'. The phrase was coined by Theodor Adorno, in his essay 'Beethoven's Late Style'. He notes that late style occurs when an artist's 'subjectivity' is so 'ruthlessly proclaiming itself' that it 'breaks through the roundedness of form for the sake of expression, exchanging harmony for the dissonance of its sorrow and spurning sensuous charm under the dictates of the imperiously emancipated mind'.[224] In this account, the artist eschews the formal perfections of their medium to explore, instead, idiosyncratic artistic desires. Edward Said has noted that Adorno's account of late style contravenes the traditional conception that an artist's late works 'reflect a special maturity' and a 'new spirit of reconciliation and maturity' associated with a 'sense of resolution'.[225] Late style opts for complexity over resolution.

Said, glossing Adorno's account, states that late style occurs 'when the artist who is fully in command of his medium nevertheless abandons communication with the established social order of which he is a part and achieves a contradictory, alienated relationship with it'.[226] From this perspective, artistic late style is an increasingly isolated approach to creative production, which seeks more to please the artist than the audience through an adherence to individual interests rather than formal unities. It is, as Said states, a 'kind of self-imposed exile from what is generally acceptable'.[227] And the style of self-exiled 'late' artists is characterised by 'intransigence, difficulty, and unresolved contradictions' that makes their works hard to pin down.[228] Yoshiki Tajiri has argued that Said's reconceptualisation of late style is accompanied by three formal qualities: 'withdrawal from the world, self-quotation, and mannerism'.[229] Self-quotation occurs when late works return to the themes, ideas, and obsessions of the earlier works in the mode of 'recollection'; mannerism refers to stylistic embellishments that 'have no particular structural function'.[230]

Murnane's late novels—in their frequent depictions of monastic living, alternate worlds, imaginary racing games, and living in remote localities—certainly depict a withdrawal from the world, even if Murnane himself is not a hermit in any meaningful sense (in point of fact, Murnane is highly social, and appears to know and chat with virtually everyone he encounters in Goroke). They also engage in a variety of mannerisms that do not have an obvious structural function: the repetition of 'image-[word]' in *A History of Books;* the obsessive numbering of sections within each novel without any clear meaning; the repetition of formal descriptions—such as the 'chief character of this work of fiction'—over simple terms like protagonist; and even the fetishisation of grammatically correct long sentences over and above agrammatical but expressive forms. And as for self-quotation, possibly no other author's body of literary work is so rigorously and relentlessly autoreferential, recycling and repurposing its own content across books in slightly altered forms. How many of Murnane's books retell the story of the girl on the train from *A Lifetime on Clouds*, or the girl in the well from *Inland*, or the imaginary racing games of *Tamarisk Row*?

Murnane's four final novels—*Barley Patch*, *A History of Books*, *A Million Windows*, and *Border Districts*—are exemplary works of late style; the only problem with this claim is that virtually all of Murnane's novels exhibit these hallmarks of lateness. One could argue that Murnane's work is only late style: every work from *The Plains* onward displays clear tendencies toward withdrawal, mannerism and self-quotation. It may be that the inherent 'lateness' of Murnane's style is due to his early struggles to get published: the restored *A Season on Earth* is one of Murnane's few works that does not seem 'late'. Perhaps this would also be true of the manuscript of *The Only Adam* or the original version of *Tamarisk Row*. The inevitable exploration of Murnane's archives will eventually shed more light on these matters.

Regardless, the final four novels intensify these 'late' qualities, as Murnane extends his stylistic tendencies as far as they can go. His deployment of self-quotation is amplified by what I have called retrospective intention. Each work seeks in some way to respond to, recover, or give coherence to his earlier work: *Barley Patch* recuperates the incomplete novel of

O, Dem Golden Slippers and fashions itself as a sequel to *Tamarisk Row; A History of Books* presents a ramified, readerly memoir that apophatically reveals his novelistic influences, and recycles scenes and events from Murnane's prior works; *A Million Windows* outlines Murnane's aesthetics and unusual novelistic methods, often with reference to his own works as illustrative examples; *Border Districts* revises the opening of *The Plains* and implicitly responds to its account of vision in order to restore the dialogic form of the unpublished *The Only Adam.*

Murnane's lateness is further emphasised through his increasing desire to inhabit an ambiguous genre of writing that cannot easily be described as either fiction or non-fiction. Essays such as 'The Breathing Author' and 'The Still-Breathing Author' seem to clarify the unusual relationship between his life and his autobiographical fiction, but in many ways only add to the ambiguity. Murnane has, however, argued against the categorisation of his work as autobiography in surprisingly practical terms:

> There are statements … that I couldn't possibly make, unless I were alone in a room in a writing sort of mood … if you challenged me with some of the statements I'd say, 'No, I don't really believe that. That's not part of my personality.' Because you must know, any of you who've tried writing … you become a different person for the time being … there are parts of you that you don't even know about yourself, until you sit down and start writing.[231]

Murnane's writing may simply be what has come to be known as 'autofiction'. This term was famously coined in the 1970s by Serge Doubrovsky, but even he defined the term in three distinct ways over his career.[232] In its contemporary form, autofiction it is often applied to work by such writers as Sheila Heti, Rachel Cusk, Karl Ove Knausgaard and Ben Lerner. I am hesitant to compare Murnane to these authors, both because he began writing many decades before them, but also because his work is so different stylistically. Nonetheless, Christian Lorentzen's definition of autofiction as distinct from 'autobiographical fiction' and 'autobiographical metafiction' seems useful here; he argues that 'in autofiction there tends to be emphasis on the narrator's or protagonist's or authorial alter ego's status as a writer or artist and that the book's creation is inscribed in the book itself'.[233] Murnane's writing, in this sense at least, would seem to constitute autofiction, because the process of composition and his status as an author is always foregrounded through the persona of the implied author. From this perspective, 'true fiction' might just be another variant of what is more commonly called autofiction. But Murnane's meta-process of framing and giving coherence to his work suggests a much more thorough process of self-fashioning than we encounter in an autofictional novel. For example, *Last Letter to an Ideal Reader* is a work of literal auto-criticism that in some way pre-empts books like this one in its desire to self-analyse Murnane's entire oeuvre. Murnane's scrupulous maintenance of his archives ensures that he will continue to influence how critics understand his work even after death.

Murnane's 'late style' may, in part, explain why his work has taken decades to find the audience it deserves. He was always destined to be a cult author, because his writing from *The Plains* onwards is so self-referential and mannered. I am often asked which of Murnane's novels readers should start with, but there is no easy point of entry (my suggestion, instead, is the short story 'When the Mice Failed to Arrive', which contains, in miniature, the major themes and techniques that he develops across his work). Responses to Murnane's work often tend to extremes: many readers, like me, become obsessed, wanting to read everything he has written, while other readers remain bemused or puzzled or worse. I will admit that, despite reading and enjoying *The Plains* when I first arrived in Australia nearly twenty years ago, I only began to appreciate Murnane's work fully after reading five of his books. This may sound like literary Stockholm syndrome, but something in those early experiences kept me reading. The devoted reader of Murnane will discover that their enjoyment only increases as they recognise the call-backs, the revisions of earlier scenes, and the belated revelation of withheld connections between earlier and later works.

Murnane's place in Australian letters seems increasingly secure. There is a growing body of scholarship on his writing. This is the third monograph dedicated to his work along with Imre Salusinszky's 1993 study of Murnane and Brendan McNamee's *Grounded Visionary* (2019), which argues that Murnane's fiction is an expression of the 'Perennial Philosophy', while also offering detailed readings of his work in chronological order. The AustLit database records 310 pieces of literary criticism on Murnane's writing, testifying to his increasing importance in Australian literature. However, it is worth noting that other major Australian writers—such as David Malouf (1102 works of literary criticism), Helen Garner (632 works), and Frank Moorhouse (461 works)—remain significantly more written about than Murnane. Murnane seems more prominent than he actually is because of his fans' devotion and their presence on social media, like Book Twitter. Murnane's reputation is also helped by the fact that he is published by a series of well-regarded international publishers, all of whom have an interest in publicising his work.

Murnane's international recognition has been belated, but the local reception of his work remains divided. Over the several years that I have been writing this book, I have regularly had other scholars and critics make jokes about Murnane's books being boring or of limited interest: 'Gerald Mundane', said one with a laugh. As someone who primarily reads fiction that could be described as 'experimental', I am both habituated and inured to these sentiments, but I have a hard time imagining any other Australian writer provoking such comments. Nonetheless, it does seem notable that even many of Murnane's fans register boredom as a crucial part of his aesthetics. Ben Lerner argues that 'Murnane's sentences are little dialectics of boredom and beauty, flatness and depth', and the pleasure of reading them derives precisely from this oscillation between tedium and visionary splendor.[234] There is a languor in his writing that makes his books both enjoyable and unique—but appreciating this requires readers to be open to unusual literary experiences.

Nicholas Birns has argued that Murnane is both 'the most Australian of writers' and 'the least Australian of writers'[235]. His geographical localism—including the fact that he has never left Australia—clashes, as Birns notes, with his cosmopolitan influences, including authors in translation from Europe and Latin America. While Murnane's content is Australian, his aesthetics comprise a localised, autodidactic variant of the international avant-garde, so it is unsurprising that Murnane's late reception has largely been international. Local enmities have probably been inflamed by international readers' and institutions' increasing interest in Murnane. Australia's sense of inadequacy about the legitimacy of its culture—a social psychological phenomenon that A.A. Phillips dubbed the 'cultural cringe'—also manifests in the 'cringe inverted' or an overcompensatory cultural patriotism[236] that can inspire a resentment of the international mediation of Australian literature. Moreover, many of these historical enmities may be linked both to personality and milieu. For example, Murnane's work was championed by the highly prolific Australian book critic, Peter Craven, who has been both an influential and a divisive figure in Melbourne literary circles. I have only ever seen Murnane be polite and affable, but he does have a track record of criticising local publishers and gatekeepers, and his archives contain many folders of his 'falling out' with various writers and friends. Joseph Steinberg recently quoted—and thereby drew my attention to—Barry Oakley's account of his friendship with Murnane. Oakley was the author who recommended Murnane's first novel, *Tamarisk Row,* to his eventual publisher, and was also an early advocate for *The Plains.* However, their relationship soured after Oakley was critical of *Inland.* Though they reconciled two decades later, Oakley argues that 'with Gerald, if you weren't an admirer you were an enemy, and now I was one'.[237] Increasingly, however, the Australian reception of Murnane's work is, if not entirely irrelevant, then certainly less significant: he has become an international author, and his reputation will be made globally.

Pascale Casanova, in *The World Republic of Letters* (2004), has usefully described this phenomenon in her account of 'national versus international writers'.[238] National writers are those who 'embody a national or popular definition of literature', while international writers are those 'who uphold an autonomous definition of literature',[239] and 'draw upon this transnational repertoire of literary techniques in order to escape being imprisoned in a national tradition'.[240] For Casanova, the exemplary international author is James Joyce who was 'rejected in Dublin' but 'lionized in Paris';[241] Murnane's work has been published almost entirely within Australia, but he has often been working against publishing trends, and his late career resurgence, as he told me, has been possible because of the unfailing support of his main publisher, Giramondo—who also have worked to encourage interest internationally. Paul Genoni has argued that Murnane should be considered 'Australia's first truly "post-national" fiction writer' because he is 'obsessively interested in aspects of the Australian landscape', but not interested in 'the processes of geo-political annexation and social enculturation by which the nation was formed'.[242] Murnane's nationalism is thus localised and topographical in Genoni's sense. While this idea is appealing, Murnane's allegorisation of Australian cultural politics in *The Plains* and *Landscape with Landscape* would seem to contradict any notion of his post-nationalism.

Murnane's work remains shadowed by a series of strong and persistent criticisms, particularly in Australia: some of these are the stylistic objections that I have already covered, but others relate to content. Perhaps no aspect of Murnane's writing has been more widely and vociferously criticised than his portrayal of gender. One scholar I know has jokingly described *The Plains* to me as 'a feminist dystopia'; Murnane himself recalls an early review of *Landscape with Landscape*, which referred to it as 'a feminist reader's nightmare'.[243] Katharine England's review from the *Adelaide Advertiser* comes close to saying this, condemning Murnane's depiction of 'plastic picture-women, defined by landscapes of skin, long blonde hair', as well as the narrators' 'sterile self-obsession', 'abrasiveness', and 'endless aggressive drinking and puking' which is 'neither amusing or laughable' but 'embarrassing and infuriating, an annoying imposition'; her overall assessment of the novel is brutal: 'very clever, very brilliant, very boring'.[244] A female scholar, who loves Murnane's work, suggested to me that one must either be a man or raised Catholic or both to enjoy his novels. Brigid Rooney has also argued that Murnane's 'yearnings directed towards ideal women' reflect how 'ritualised gestures' are 'transmuted in writing' even after 'faith in Catholic dogma evaporates'.[245] Susan Lever, in a review of Salusinszky's book on Murnane in 1993, argued that Murnane's 'critique of male Catholicism contains a fair chunk of celebration' and that Murnane's work positions the female 'reader as she who should be suffocated and silenced'.[246] Sue Gillet has argued that the female characters in Murnane's early fiction are reduced to being 'the signifier of the relationships between these males' in ways that implicitly objectify them.[247] Salusinszky has countered that Murnane's portrayals are more radical than the claims of '"male feminists" who have repeatedly moralised against his daring to represent male sexuality in some of its many versions',[248] but this feels like an insufficient response that glosses over the reasons why this criticism is so pervasive. I want to consider the portrayal of gender in Murnane in order to contextualise the way it is deployed in his work. My point here is neither to judge Murnane's depiction of gender, nor to offer apologetics for it, but simply to understand it. This strikes me as a necessary first step, and one that most criticisms and defenses of Murnane have skipped over.

Although it was written before Murnane's return to writing, Ken Gelder and Paul Salzman have offered a representative example of the critique of Murnane's portrayal of gender, citing his 'depiction of women as rather old-fashioned Muses, empty vessels waiting to be filled by male desire.'[249] It is worth subjecting this claim to some scrutiny, because this is certainly not the case with all or even most of the women in Murnane's fiction; consider, for example, the depiction of Murnane's aunt who left the convent in *Barley Patch*. She is neither idealised nor sexualised, and seems to be a perfectly rounded (and flawed) character hardly inscribed by male desire. But Gelder and Salzman are correct in suggesting, as I read it here, that women in Murnane's fiction are frequently subjected to an objectifying 'male gaze', which Laura Mulvey famously described as the cinematic production of the 'image of woman as (passive) raw material for the (active) gaze of man'.[250] Their criticism that

Murnane's fiction often depicts women as ciphers or objects on whom the male narrators project meaning is correct in many cases, as when the narrator of *The Plains* waits by a window to look at the daughter of his patron walking across the yard, and notes that her 'figure was never quite distinct from the shadowy after-images of whatever I had been reading'.[251] As Daniel Davis Wood argues, some 'readers will find they can't stomach yet another male protagonist objectifying a woman',[252] but the male gaze in Murnane's novels is often deployed in critical and self-reflexive ways that require analysis.

Imre Salusinszky argues that Murnane's fiction draws on a literary tradition that 'probably begins with Dostoievski's *Notes from Underground*' in which 'a young, alienated male narrator is trapped in some kind of indecision or guilt'.[253] He argues that Murnane's fiction critically explores 'male sexual conditioning' in all of its various guises and potential unpleasantness, including 'its intensity, its confusion, its violence, and above all its hilarious misfirings'.[254] He also notes a change between the early works, which are often explicit in their sexual fantasies, and the later works where sexuality is abstracted into 'the abyss of otherness that separates all minds'[255] and takes on an increasingly ambiguous and philosophical meaning. Daniel Davis Wood argues that 'Murnane's typical protagonist is a man who objectifies a woman. But at no stage is this man under the illusion that the woman he objectifies is available to him'.[256] This lack of availability is a key issue because, for the typical Murnanian protagonist, women 'are objects that inspire carnal desires which he doesn't know how to answer' as a result 'of his cultural background'.[257] The cultural background, in Murnane's case, is a puritanical strain of Catholicism as it was practiced in Australia in the 1940s and 50s. Not only did Murnane's childhood religion demonise sexuality and sexual curiosity, but it also placed men and women into distinct and separate social roles that discouraged their interaction.

Murnane's fiction often calls attention to the way that gendered divisions of labour and socialisation are policed. In *Barley Patch,* for example, the enforced social separation of genders reappears throughout the novel: the separation of children at school into boys and girls rooms, the preparation of Sunday meals in his aunt's house only undertaken by women, the breeding cages that separate male and female birds, the figure of Aunt Bee who disapproves of the narrator's interest in the young female character in *Brat Farrar*, and, of course, the narrator's own interest in his girl-cousins' doll house which is discouraged for gendered reasons. Elsewhere, Murnane's fiction foregrounds participation in domestic spheres traditionally associated with female forms of immaterial labour: 'I used to stay at home to mind my son and my daughter and to do the housework while my wife was away at her job'.[258] This fictionalised situation reflects real experiences as a 'house husband' in the late 1970s: 'My wife had been confined to the house with our three small sons for four years and wanted to resume her career. I was used to helping with housework and shopping and child minding'.[259] These depictions arguably prefigure more recent literary works—such as Karl Ove Knausgaard's *My Struggle*—that have examined male experiences in the domestic sphere.

The appearance of idealised female characters in Murnane's novels are also a frequent source of criticism. Consider

Murnane's 'Patroness' or 'Ideal Reader' who seems influenced by a Marist Christian tradition as well as the Dantean tradition of the idealised muse (Beatrice) who guides the poet. But idealised women in Murnane novels are hardly representations of purity, and often are closer in character to the Patroness: a projection of a female personage who understands the narrator and must be posited or idealised because no real counterpart exists. To put it another way, the female characters are distant and idealised because of the protagonists' loneliness and separation—often a result of gendered social structures—that discourage male and female interaction. Samantha Trayhurn has argued that 'Murnane's ideal female reader becomes an embodiment of all that Murnane cannot know or understand about the opposite sex' and thus offers a means by which he might 'venture beyond the limits of his own mind';[260] if we accept Trayhurn's claim here, then the idealisation of the Ideal Reader constitutes an attempt to understand (perhaps poorly) rather than simply to objectify.

While Murnane's fiction definitively employs the male gaze, the gaze itself is often subjected to self-reflexive and historically informed criticism, as in this passage from *Inland,* where the adolescent narrator encounters nude paintings in a book entitled *Famous Artists:*

> The nudes repelled me. The skin of the women was yellowish; their bodies were too plump. The fabrics beneath the reclining bodies were too richly crimson or purple, and the carefully arranged wrinkles in the fabric made me resent the wealth and power of the men of Europe who

> could order their female servants to pose naked for hours and afterwards to set in order the same vast beds that earlier they had been commanded to disarrange artfully and then to sprawl their interesting but lumpish bodies on.[261]

Here, the narrator's male gaze comes into contact with the material manifestation of the male gaze in Western painting. While the narrator's gaze is still objectifying in its description of the women's 'yellowish' skin and 'plump' bodies, his experience is repulsion rather than attraction or arousal. But the experience of the objectifying gaze then unexpectedly turns into a material critique of 'the wealth and power of the men of Europe' who are able to subjugate women for their own pleasure. But this critical insight does not develop into a feminist critique of the male gaze or even a rejection of these same subjugated women as potential sites of pleasure, since the narrator returns to their 'interesting but lumpish bodies'. While this final description is objectifying, it also seems intentionally free of obvious sexual resonance. The female bodies are 'interesting' insofar as the narrator is (apparently) ignorant of many of the most basic aspects of anatomy and sexuality, but do not create desire within him.

This passage is a good example of the way that gender, sexuality and desire are presented in Murnane's novels. They might constitute what could be termed a critical masculinity insofar as they do self-reflexively examine male desire and even historicise the male gaze and its relationship to power. Moreover, Murnane's fiction often obsessively fixates on and portrays masculine tendencies that are abject: his characters are often loners, losers, wallflowers, masturbators, perverts, and peeping toms. The novels seem to relish parading these dismal figures—almost as a totemic way of warding off their existence. As Wood states, Murnane's characters are 'often juvenile, puerile, sometimes sordid' and their 'frank descriptions of the private titillations' suggest the kind of person 'who aspires to become an Australian Jack Kerouac but ends up coming across as the Catholic answer to Alexander Portnoy'.[262] These novels, in short, satirise the anxieties of a beta-male masculinity, but this suspicion does not lead to feminist critiques of patriarchy, nor could Murnane's critical masculinity be readily recuperated within a feminist framework. But this also does not mean that his novels ignore misogyny. Male violence against women, including sexual assault, is discussed and deplored in several of Murnane's novels, such as *Inland* and *A Million Windows*, in far more direct terms than in most contemporary Australian novels. Murnane's works are also perhaps surprising in discussing and acknowledging non-heteronormative modes of desire: 'The boy himself often fell in love—mostly with girls of his own age but often with young women and sometimes with young men'.[263] Many passages in *Tamarisk Row*, in particular, examine Clement's extensive sexual curiosity about other boys.

Finally, any criticism of Murnane's use of gender must also consider the question of genre: his writing is essentially fictionalised autobiography. The occasional complaint about the lack of viewpoint female characters in his novels ignores the fact that there are virtually no internal characters in Murnane's fiction aside from the autobiographical figure of the implied author; Helen Daniel has argued that Clement, the protagonist of *Tamarisk Row*, effectively becomes the narrator of all of Murnane's subsequent novels.[264] These narrators who resemble Murnane share not only his gender, but also his age, nationality, upbringing, religious background, and tendencies toward intense rumination and imaginative games. The problem, if that's what it is, is that Murnane's writing contains no viewpoint characters who are not Gerald Murnane. This would be a limitation for a novelist, but if we view Murnane, instead, as primarily an autobiographical writer, then the question of viewpoint characters seems both determined by and consistent with his genre. Examining non-viewpoint characters suggests a more complex story, since many of these female characters are rounded and have varying degrees of agency.

Murnane's artistic project seeks to represent, in great detail, his specific perspective on the world, rather than to represent a diversity of voices or imagined perspectives. Murnane's perspectives tend, as would be expected, to represent a particular embodied mode of masculine, heterosexual desire, albeit in an often critical and self-reflexive way. Many claims of Murnane's misogyny are reductive and not sufficiently attentive to the complex ways that gender is represented in his work, but this does not mean they are incorrect; as Declan Fry has stated—the tendency toward 'idealising women can be difficult to distinguish from objectification',[265] and Murnane's fiction ultimately does both, regardless of how complex or ironic this objectification might be. The contents of Murnane's archives may only stir up further controversy about his tendencies toward objectification, given that there are files entitled '3000 Words about Naked Females' and 'more than 1000 Illustrations of Naked Women Removed from Girlie Magazines and Marked with Coloured Stickers to Explain My Reasons for Preserving Them'.[266] The combination of objectification, obsession, and excessive self-analysis here is hard to disambiguate; Oakley—upon receiving these descriptions from Murnane—called them 'both extraordinary and somewhat disturbing'.[267] Nonetheless, despite the stereotypical claim that Murnane's readers are only men, it seems notable that many of Murnane's most significant critics are women, including Helen Daniel, Carmel Bird, Merve Emre and Brigid Rooney.

Another frequent claim about Murnane's work—which often amounts to a criticism, though it should not be—is the idea that either Murnane or his fiction are in some way autistic. An anonymous review of Murnane's *Collected Fictions* in *Kirkus Reviews* argues that his fiction is often 'tiresome, with a style that sounds like a government report written by a bureaucrat with mild Asperger's', and a 'forced flatness'. In two radio interviews on ABC National, Ramona Koval has—without malice, though not particularly sensitively—suggested to Murnane that writing about 'feelings of being a little bit separate from the world and making lists and making lots of categories' might be a 'slightly autistic way to be in the world'.[268] Murnane responded politely saying 'I might be that way', but quickly qualified this answer noting that, when authors reveal as much about themselves in their writing as Murnane has, then perhaps others can see 'fault lines and peculiar knots of qualities in your own personality'; he goes on to discuss the '*moi profond*' or deep self in Proust, stating that 'perhaps an autistic version of me ... does my writing, but ... I'm communicating well enough with you'.[269]

Elsewhere, however, Murnane has rejected the notion entirely, and suggested that Koval's comments are a kind of class prejudice: because Murnane doesn't 'go to parties, travel on aeroplanes' or 'love the South of France and drinking wine' then he must be 'autistic or something else'; Burns quotes Murnane's friend, Kate James, who argues that 'Gerald isn't nearly as eccentric as people like to pretend he is', but he 'gets labelled as an eccentric because he's not the same as most Australian academics and intellectuals' and 'doesn't care about status; he's way too honest'.[270] Murnane makes it clear in Burns's essay that he does not identify in any way as autistic.

For those of us who are readers of Murnane and neurodivergent, however, there are aspects of his writing that do seem to reflect these experiences in positive and interesting ways, whether it is the account of intense and detailed fantasies, the intricate obsessions, the nigh-anthropological analysis directed at understanding normative human behaviour, the frequent fear of losing control of emotions and executive functioning (which are described as 'nervous breakdowns'), or even the manner in which his writing can veer—with so little change in its rhetoric or tone—from the deeply serious to the highly irreverent. It is perhaps tempting to read these as aesthetic affects that approximate neurodivergence, but such an approach seems both reductive and perhaps dangerously essentialising. Moreover, having obsessions, fantasies and feeling like an outsider are all nearly universal human experiences, and unrequited love, which is perhaps Murnane's signature subject, may be among the oldest topics in literature. It is possible to write sensitively and positively about autism as a literary mode of affect, and Amanda Tink's recent essay '"Nearly all deep fertile soil": Les Murray, His Son and Autism' presents one excellent Australian model of this, but this example is different because of Murray's self-identification with autism in the poem.

The other problem with this identification is that it rests on the notion that the narratorial personas in Murnane's work are an actual reflection of him, rather than a carefully constructed artifice. I have only interacted with Gerald Murnane personally on a handful of occasions, and only once for an extended period. I do not claim to know him well, or what he is like in his day-to-day life, though the man I encountered was gregarious, generous, precise, and very funny. Thankfully, we do not need to know Murnane to be able to analyse the self-fashioning occurring in his work, because we can compare his very different methods of self-fashioning in another body of his writing: his poetry. Murnane's poetry is different from his fiction: it is comparatively direct, unadorned, confessional, and sometimes sentimental. Shannon Burns has described Murnane's prosaic narrators as 'almost totally deadpan'[271] but his poetic ones are comparatively earnest. The 'deadpan' nature of Murnane's narrators is not some intrinsic authorial trait, but an intentional aesthetic effect: one of the joys of this deadpan narration is that the narrator can make sudden and dramatic shifts in tone without changing the rhetoric of the text, and the careless reader might miss these changes altogether.

Murnane may provoke such reactions because—as a homemade avant-garde of one—his work is so unusual. His formal education comprised a teaching qualification and later a BA undertaken at night school as a mature student. He had virtually no engagement with literary institutions early in his life, and there was little in the way of local literary culture to support his unusual reading habits. He discusses how he had to read international papers, such as the *Times Literary Supplement*, to discover new fiction and often had to place these books on special order, also from overseas. But despite these challenges, or perhaps because of them, he has produced a series of works that blur genre distinctions between fiction and non-fiction, and which engage with and respond to each other in complex ways. His books are beautifully written, theoretically complex and emotionally charged in a way that rewards rereading. His style might appear static or formal at times, but this belies the wide range of aesthetic effects that he can produce. He is without question both the most original and most significant Australian author of the last fifty years, and the best writer Australia has produced since Christina Stead. This claim will be hotly contested by many—and perhaps most—Australian critics and readers, but I suspect it will become a commonplace sentiment internationally.

Murnane has often been compared to minimalist composers, such as Phillip Glass and Steve Reich, but the artist he most reminds me of is Joseph Cornell, the New York artist famous for creating his detailed boxed assemblages out of found materials sourced from secondhand stores and opportunity shops. Like Murnane, Cornell was deeply influenced by the avant-garde (particularly Expressionism and Surrealism), but he was almost entirely self-taught and his understanding of art history was both autodidactic and idiosyncratic. Like Murnane, Cornell was famous for his organisation and filing systems.

Just as Murnane has rarely left the state of Victoria and has never left Australia, Cornell almost never left New York City, and never travelled overseas, despite being profoundly interested in other countries and other places (again, much like Murnane). Cornell made the majority of his mature artworks in the basement of his mother's house, and Murnane is famous for typing his works at the kitchen bench and on top of an ironing board in his spare room. There are differences, of course: Cornell never married or had children. Cornell's complex fear of and attraction to women—including the obsessive recording of his own voyeurism—is also well documented. But Cornell's assemblages, like Murnane's writings, are simultaneously homemade and deeply personal—yet also somehow wholly self-sufficient and autonomous creations that make the viewer feel as if they are peering into a new and unknown world. Murnane's fiction produces a similar effect: the specificity of his narrator's perspective and the often-overwhelming detail of experience makes the window of his vision narrow, but its horizonal depth feels endless. Murnane's fiction differs from Cornell's art in its cumulative effect: it would be as if, in lining up all of Cornell's boxes end-to-end, one discovered a new and previously undisclosed macroscopic work of art.

For all of its strangeness, Murnane's work is still invested in recognisable and traditional literary notions of the beautiful and the sublime—and he repeatedly suggests that reading and writing are privileged ways for accessing these transcendent moments. *A History of Books* ends with a passage that exemplifies the intertextual sublimity of Murnane's work. The narrator describes the hypothetical ending of a novel that a man—who appears to be a past self of the narrator—wished to write. This ending (which, oddly, is not his ideal ending, but his second choice) would reflect his own mental state upon finishing his reading of a novel thirty years earlier. Neither text nor author are named, and the ending's content is only vaguely described. As Murnane notes in 'The Still Breathing Author', the work referred to is Halldór Laxness's *World Light*, which concludes with a poet, Ólafur Kárason, walking away over a glacier into the light of dawn, as he simultaneously recalls watching the ocean as a small child; the last sentence, set off as its own paragraph, is an ecstatic, almost religious exhortation: 'And beauty shall reign alone'.[272] The narrator of *A History of Books* literally—albeit obliquely—rewrites the ending of *World Light* in abstract terms:

> The chief character in a certain work of fiction had seemed to pass from sight in a place where the white seemed to meet, or even to merge, with the blue; where the land seemed to meet, or even to merge, with the sky, the visible with the invisible, the writer even with the reader, and whatever had been written with whatever had been read.[273]

Just as Ólafur quite literally disappears in the morning light on the glacier, Murnane imagines a character disappearing in the hazy indistinction of the horizon. The merging of the white and blue (and it is interesting here to recall that *Border Districts* similarly ends with a 'stained whiteness') reflects Laxness's contrast between the white of the glacier and the implicit blue of both the ocean in Ólafur's memory and the sky beyond the glacier. What Murnane prizes is this moment of merging, which is reflected formally as the ending of *World Light* becomes the rewritten hypothetical ending for an imagined novel that has now become the actual ending of *A History of Books.* It is an apophatic moment that is profoundly spiritual in its sense of striving for something higher beyond the self. But it is also about the power of literature itself, which derives from the intimate communion between writer and reader.

Late Recognition: An Interview with Gerald Murnane

This review was conducted in the Men's Shed in Goroke in October of 2019. Murnane had recently won—for the first time—a major Australian prize for a novel, when *Border Districts* received the Prime Minister's Literary Award in late 2018. The long piece on Murnane in *The New York Times Magazine* by Mark Binelli had appeared the previous year, and the national news program, *The 7.30 Report,* had run a segment on Murnane's work and his life in Goroke. These media stories evidenced the increasing esteem that his work was held in both internationally and nationally—though these accolades also clashed notably with the comparatively humble circumstances of his life. It seemed like an opportune time to ask Murnane questions about the way that his work had been valued, and what this late recognition meant to him. I was particularly interested to get his views on how the internet had in many ways propelled his status—since much of the buzz around Murnane's work had developed online over the last ten years in blogs, on social media like Twitter, and on social reading sites like Goodreads. Although Murnane has famously never used a computer, he does use a mobile phone and has admitted that 'my vanity drives me sometimes to google my name followed by the word *author* and to feel proud of the sheer number of reviews of my books and articles or essays about them'.[274] I was curious to see whether and to what degree he was aware of the way that digital technology had supported the reception of his work.

The internet appeared during the period when you had quit writing. I know you are not a computer user, but do you have a sense whether it has helped your reputation? Do you think it's connected your fans to one another?

In the past, books themselves were a sort of internet. Some bloke would write to me from California and say, 'I found a second-hand copy of *Landscape with Landscape* in a bookshop in San Francisco. It's an amazing book.' And I thought, how did it get there? But he's read it and he has written to me, so I knew this was happening. The intensity and the sheer volume of what happens now, though, I cannot comprehend. I get inklings of it. The other day I said to Ivor [Indyk, Publisher at Giramondo], 'Things are pretty quiet now after the big event on my eightieth birthday.' And he said, 'They are never really quiet. If you could see what's being said about you on social media, you would be highly gratified.'

I don't like thinking about it. It's a bit like my primitive feelings—and this is going to amuse you—about my calculator.

When I'm doing calculations with random numbers and probabilities in the racing world [in Murnane's racing game known as the 'Antipodean Archive'], I only input numbers up to three decimal places, so it doesn't strain the calculator. I have this primitive awe of the internet. Every night before I go to bed, I wipe out all of my phone conversations. I have only two friends whose conversations I keep, because I don't want to put too much of a strain on my pet machine. So, I have only a primitive sense that there are words about me flying around from one tower to another. The amazing thing about this latter-day fame—and I do not want to seem ungrateful—is that my writing hardly changed. It was the attitude of readers that changed.

You have many overseas fans of your work, including some notable US writers, many of whom could read you because your books had been published there and existed in used book shops, which was certainly the case for The Plains. *How did* The Plains *come to be published in the US?*

The Plains was first published in America in 1985 by George Braziller. Poor old George, whom I never met, put his heart and soul and lots of his money into the promotion of that book. It pretty well sank without a trace, as far as I know. I think this was largely the result of one review in *Publishers Weekly*, which I've got a copy of. The key words in it were 'philosophical treatise'. I used to say, well, imagine it's a cold Friday afternoon in Wichita, Kansas. You are the leading bookseller in town and no-one is in the shop at the moment, so you get out *Publishers Weekly* and see if you can find six recent novels to buy.

And skimming through those, you see these words 'philosophical treatise', and just keep going. I imagine that was what happened in bookshops all over the United States. That was the end of *The Plains* in America. I was told afterwards that it rocked Braziller's confidence: he thought this book was going to do well, but his judgment seemed astray.

It was published again by a small publisher at the University of South Michigan in a place called Kalamazoo. The reasons for these things always go back to one person: in this case, a young Fulbright Scholar, whose name escapes me, who came to Australia in the early 90s and became enthusiastic about my work. He got an academic post at a university in Georgia and he prevailed on an editor friend of his at this university press in Kalamazoo to do an edition of *The Plains*. Things went wrong from the start. The editor became unwell and left the press, and they didn't publicise the book. I don't even know how I got a copy. I know that it was published, but whether it even got distributed I wouldn't have a clue. I thought those were my two chances, and I wouldn't get a third.

Well, this man called Jeremy Davis sent me a letter around about 2012 after I had moved to Goroke. In the letter, he said he had never been so moved by a work of fiction as he had been moved by *Inland*. And I felt very appreciative of that. *Inland* is the book that I put the most feeling into. I have ways of describing or categorising my books. The book I put the most thought into, in the sense of theoretical thinking, was *A Million Windows*. I regard *A Million Windows* as more important than *The Plains*, but *The Plains* was the one that made my reputation.

Anyway, Jeremy Davies at that time was at a small press called The Dalkey Archive and he published *Inland* and then *Barley Patch.* Neither of those books—for whatever reason—was successful at all. Again, I thought, OK, that's it. I am never going to be successful in the United States, certainly not in my lifetime. Then Jeremy moved to Farrar, Straus and Giroux in New York—the Parnassus of world publishing. And then Mark Binelli came out from *The New York Times* and he had actually read several of my books and we got on very well. I tend to get on well with most people who like my books. It's like they've decided already that I couldn't be too bad a bloke. Well, Mark Binelli wrote his long piece about me, and the Americans discovered me at last, you might say.

You've spoken in the past about your often fraught relationship with publishers, who have asked you to change your work, especially earlier in your career. How has that been different over the later part of your career?

I have cautioned people before: don't you dare to suppose that I simply sat down with a program of writing at the age of twenty-five, and then had book after book published without a hitch. While I was writing every book, I was aware that my current publisher might not like it or might publish it grudgingly. *Emerald Blue* failed because the publisher couldn't be bothered publicising it. So my book suffered as a result. It irked me when people would ask me, 'What are you writing now?' Well, there's not much point in me telling you what I'm writing, if it's not certain to be published!

The turning point in my career was when Ivor Indyk kept pestering me at this conference [on Murnane's work] in Newcastle in the week when the buildings were destroyed in New York. I'd never met Ivor, but I had sent him things for his magazine, *HEAT*. He came up and said, 'Could you send me a copy of your speech, "The Breathing Author" and I'll publish it?' And that led to his publishing *Invisible Yet Enduring Lilacs*. The feeling that I had a sympathetic publisher at last at the age of sixty—that helped in no small way to generate the books that followed.

So was Barley Patch *written with the knowledge that Giramondo would publish it?*

Not only that, but it was written after I'd been working on this thing called, *O, Dem Golden Slippers* and I had lost confidence in myself. I've lost confidence in myself several times over the years: not in the sense that I couldn't write what I wanted to write and very well, but that I couldn't write anything that people would publish. Because of *Emerald Blue*'s failure—and it was a commercial failure—I doubted if *O, Dem Golden Slippers* was publishable. If I had taken it in a synopsis form to any publisher, I think they would have just politely told me to take it somewhere else. And that was the feeling I had all through those silent years when I was working on my horse-racing archive rather than writing. *Barley Patch* is not really a book so much as it as an explanation as to why another book wasn't written, that book being *O, Dem Golden Slippers*.

With *Barley Patch*, I knew the whole time that I probably had a publisher for it. I felt liberated and grateful for the opportunity to rewrite a book that I thought could have been of enormous merit, but which got out of control. Still, I don't want you to think that Ivor automatically accepted whatever I wrote. For example, he objected once to my using a reference to masturbation, and I went off at him about it. We had our occasional differences.

Perhaps *O, Dem Golden Slippers* got out of control because I thought it would be hard to find a publisher, and I could almost say, ah, who cares? I have taken many wrong turns. If I just gave you the merest glimpse into my literary archives, where there's a drawer for each of my books, you'd see false beginnings and wrong turnings and abandoned ideas. Even in *Landscape with Landscape*, which began as a collection of short stories, there were two fairly sizable pieces that were left out: 'Her Skin Can Stand the Closest Inspection', which was a reference to an old ad for luxury soap, and another long piece. In fact, there's a whole drawer at the end of my archives, the sixteenth drawer, which is labelled 'Unpublished or Unfinished'.

You are arguably the most prominent living Australian author not to have won the Miles Franklin Award. How do you feel about literary awards?

Shannon Burns wrote a piece deploring the state of literary prizes because *A Million Windows* wasn't listed for a single award. This justifies my view—and this is true of any field—that it is fashion rather than judgment that determines these awards. And I will say in support of this, that I have written many better books than *Border Districts*, which won the Prime Minister's Literary Award for Fiction after the Americans had discovered me. People have explained to me that *Border Districts* is a much more complicated book than it seems, and maybe as a more skillful writer, I didn't notice the skill and effort that went into producing it. It is a better book than I am currently giving it credit for, but I never expected it to win. Which of my more recent books deserved to win? *A Million Windows.* My books have seldom been fashionable enough to win major awards, but I've been given awards for lifetime achievement, the Patrick White Award and an Emeritus Award from the Literature Board of the Australia Council.

When we were talking earlier, you mentioned that you thought two of your most important books were A Million Windows *and* Inland. *What was the reception of* Inland *like?*

The first review in Australia was completely uncomprehending, and said I'd turned to postmodernism or something like that. And the book got a very confused review from someone in the *Times Literary Supplement*. I tried to explain *Inland* to somebody who had bought the film rights to it. Now if there was an insane filmmaker who wanted to take on the hardest of my books to film, he would have taken on *Inland.* This was a young man, who bought a three-year option. He was a Tasmanian who'd only made documentaries. And this young filmmaker started writing to me, and a couple of things he said convinced me of what I suspected all along—that he hadn't the faintest idea what *Inland* was about. So, I started writing to him about the meaning of *Inland*. But after about three quarters of a page, I realised that I wasn't on the right track. I don't think even I know what it's about!

If you can imagine a person reading a book and becoming so greatly affected by the book that he decides—as difficult as it seems—that he is going to get inside that book so that he can meet on equal terms with a character, his dream girl—then that's the idea, in simple terms. Now that word 'character' is just used for the sake of convenience. I try never to use that word when I'm talking about fiction. I prefer the term 'personages', which I use often in *A Million Windows*. Anyway, the reader of the book wants to get on equal terms with this personage, but you can't be on equal terms when you are simply reading. He can only do it through some miracle or disturbance in the world as we know it, and he finds himself writing a book as a way of doing this. All this is made possible by the Institute of Prairie Studies and Anne Kristaly Gunnarsen, an editor. It's hard to explain, but I will have one more try: a kid asked in class, 'Can God make a stone so heavy he can't lift it?' Well, my dream was to write a text so complicated that I couldn't understand it. *Inland* is that text.

The other text of mine that fulfils a similar role is my racing archive. I was reading last night through the results of some races, and thought: I don't even remember those races, and yet I devised and recorded them. This, to me, is just dream-happiness. You can create something that is enough to satisfy you. You don't have to posit someone else. I don't need God or another writer to create these things, because I can do it myself.

So the unfinished novel, O, Dem Golden Slippers *is named after a song. Do you know who actually performed the one you recalled from childhood?*

I heard a male chorus while I listened to a scratchy old record in a room with golden motes of dust. You can read about a similar scene in *Barley Patch.* Because I am a congenital anosmatic—I was born without a sense of smell—colour gives me a huge amount of meaning, and I visualise so many things in shades of colour. I can see in my mind the difference between purple, violet, lavender, mauve—right across a range. It takes an effort, but I can do it. My memories of the song are black and gold memories—black gloom, gold dust-motes, black singers, golden slippers, black record, gold label.

Black and gold are not colors that I normally would choose myself as racing colors, but they are the official colors of a race club called the Midlands Turf Club in New Arcady [in Murnane's 'Antipodean Archive'] and when the members of the Midlands Turf Club are issued their membership badges, they're always black and gold. There is a mention at the end of *Barley Patch* of a woman wearing black and gold, who is linked to the woman in New Arcady in the archives, and that woman, believe it or not, is connected to Catherine Earnshaw in *Wuthering Heights*. Everything of value that should have gone into *O, Dem Golden Slippers,* went into *Barley Patch.* The catch phrase that ended many sections in *O, Dem Golden Slippers,* was 'mostly level, grassy countryside with a line of trees in the distance'. I had this idea—not properly formed—of the reader getting some impression at the end of the book that it had been written entirely by someone in a nonexistent country.

In Tamarisk Row, *Clement has a namesake horse, Clementia, who is a stayer—he comes from behind to win the race. In* Something for the Pain, *you reveal that you also had a namesake horse. Are you maybe the namesake of Clementia? Are you a literary stayer with this belated international recognition of your work?*

There's this Hungarian proverb: *Ami késik, az nem múlik*—'What comes late, doesn't pass away'. My first books had their admirers. *The Plains* was highly praised. But I was never a fashionable writer, and *Emerald Blue,* for example, was almost ignored. Now, I'm told my books are discussed all over social media, which I know nothing about. Yes, I hit the front late in the race.

I'm glad it happened this way. My head would have swelled if my recent fame had come to me too soon. My head would have swelled, and I might have thought I had found the formula for success as a writer. Thank God, that didn't happen and I went on writing what I was driven to write—what I alone could write.

The intensity—or just the volume—of the fan mail is a good indicator and it reached its apogee after *The Australian* published a shortened version of Binelli's piece in *The New York Times*. Some journalists need this approach—how could a guy so well-known overseas live in Goroke? I think in some people's minds it just went like this: how did we overlook this guy? The Americans think he's great, so we must be wrong about him.

When I bought my copy of Tamarisk Row, *it had this newspaper clipping inside—here it is—and it's declaring you a national treasure back in 1986. So you have always had your supporters also, I guess?*

John Tittensor was an early supporter. He was a secondary school teacher writing reviews for a small, leftwing journal called *Nation Review.* This was back in the 70s when we had no Sunday newspapers. And he reviewed *Tamarisk Row.* He called it the best book of fiction to have appeared in Australia for a decade, but no one else went so far as that. That newspaper clipping you referenced was dated 1986—after *The Plains* had been published and praised. The first man who picked up *The Plains,* and probably started the ball rolling, was Paul Carter. He went on ABC one night, and said that *The Plains* was a masterpiece. Then he wrote about it a few weeks later and said 'time will tell if *The Plains* is a masterpiece…' Even he wouldn't stick his neck out too far.

A lot of your books talk about other books you have read as a child where you imagined things that occurred at the edges of the real narrative. Was that shaped at all by having more limited access to books than we do now?

I will give equal weight to three propositions, the first of which is the one you mentioned just now. The second reason was the sheer disappointment that the book didn't go on—that it had to end. The third was my natural urge away from the solid world into this other world of fluidity and endless possibilities. I think if I had been supplied with an abundance of books, I still would have been driven to write because the books I wanted weren't there: I had to try to write them. Many of Clement's daydreams in *Tamarisk Row* were the ones that occupied me as a boy. The passage where he looks into the orange door: I actually did that.

Nowadays, I am very hard to please as a reader. I am very strict like that now with books. I will not give up the time to read something I don't like. I am eighty years of age and I have written fifteen books. I have written my heart out almost literally, and my interests have moved somewhat. Well, my interests have never changed, but the expression of those interests has changed, and they go on without my writing about them, though I am still filling the archives.

Notes

1 Salusinszky, p. 2.
2 Coetzee, n.p.
3 Murnane, *Velvet Waters*, p. 88.
4 Trayhurn, p. 39.
5 Murnane, *Velvet Waters*, p. 74.
6 Ibid, p. 92.
7 Murnane, *Last Letter to a Reader*, p. 85.
8 Ibid.
9 Rooney, p. 69.
10 Uhlmann, 'Introduction', p. 1.
11 Burns, 'Truth, Fiction, and True Fiction', p. 29.
12 Murnane, *Last Letter*, p. 11.
13 Klee, p. 149.
14 Murnane, 'Three Archives of Gerald Murnane', p. 18.
15 Murnane, 'The Breathing Author', *Invisible Yet Enduring Lilacs*, p. 162.
16 Binelli, n.p.
17 Murnane, *Green Shadows and Other Poems*, p. 66.
18 Burns, 'The Scientist of His Own Experience', n.p.
19 Ibid.
20 Murnane, 'The Breathing Author', *Invisible Yet Enduring Lilacs*, p. 158.
21 Ibid., pp. 158–63.
22 Kenner, p. 12.
23 England.
24 Gelder, p. 51.
25 Ibid., p. 50.
26 Ibid., p. 50.
27 Binelli, n.p.
28 Steinberg, 'Review', p. 3.
29 Murnane, *Green Shadows*, p. 116.
30 Ibid., pp. 2, 23, 23, and 47.

31 Gelder and Salzman, p. 131.
32 Birns, 'Reading Gerald Murnane', p. 4.
33 Murnane, *Something for the Pain*, p. 246.
34 White, p. 39.
35 Genoni, p. 3.
36 Uhlmann, 'Introduction', p. 2.
37 Foster, n.p.
38 Murnane, *Emerald Blue*, pp. 185, 216.
39 Murnane, *Barley Patch*, p. 248.
40 Ibid. p. 248.
41 Murnane, *Invisible Yet Enduring Lilacs*, p. i.
42 Murnane, *Barley Patch*, p. 3.
43 Ibid., 82.
44 Rooney, p. 71.
45 Murnane, *Barley Patch*, p. 100.
46 Rooney, p. 68.
47 Rilke, p. 20.
48 Ibid., pp. 16–17
49 Emre, p. 253.
50 Ibid., p. 11.
51 Ibid., p. 2.
52 Murnane, *Last Letter to a Reader*, p. 12.
53 Emre, p. 4.
54 Ibid., pp. 15–16.
55 Ibid., p. 15.
56 Ibid.
57 Ibid., p. 16.
58 Murnane, *Barley Patch*, p. 98.
59 Murnane, *Last Letter*, p. 17.
60 Emre, p. 93.
61 Murnane, *Barley Patch*, p. 6.
62 Ibid., p. 24.
63 Ibid., p. 14.
64 Ibid., p. 62.
65 Ibid., p. 47.
66 Ibid., p. 47.
67 Ibid., p. 48.
68 Ibid., p. 49.
69 Ibid.
70 Murnane, 'In Praise of the Long Sentence', p. 56.
71 Ibid., p. 62.

72 Sterne, p. 380.
73 Ibid., 62.
74 Murnane, 'In Praise of the Long Sentence', p. 57.
75 Ibid., 65.
76 Gelder and Salzman, p. 131.
77 Murnane, *Barley Patch,* p. 46.
78 Ibid., p. 20.
79 Ibid., p. 21.
80 Ibid., p. 22.
81 Ibid., p. 23.
82 Ibid., p. 22.
83 Murnane, *Velvet Waters,* p. 139.
84 Murnane, *Barley Patch,* p. 189.
85 Ibid. p. 200.
86 Murnane, 'The Three Archives of Gerald Murnane', p. 18.
87 Murnane, *A Season on Earth,* p. 371.
88 Murnane, *Barley Patch,* p. 205.
89 Murnane, 'Catherine Murnane', p. 6.
90 Murnane, *Barley Patch,* p. 208.
91 Ibid., p. 252.
92 Ibid., 250.
93 Murnane, 'In Praise of the Long Sentence', p. 57.
94 Murnane, *Barley Patch,* p. 68.
95 Murnane, *A History of Books,* p. 13.
96 Birns, 'Review', p. 222.
97 Murnane, *A History of Books,* p. 51.
98 Ibid., p. 21.
99 Ibid.
100 Ibid., p. 22.
101 Ibid., pp. 23–4.
102 Ibid., p. 206.
103 Murnane, *Inland,* p. 169, italics Murnane's.
104 Murnane, *A History of Books,* p. 107.
105 Birns, 'Review', p. 223.
106 Murnane, 'The Three Archives of Gerald Murnane', p. 17.
107 Burns, 'An Idiot in a Greek Sense', n.p.
108 Steinberg, 'Signposts', n.p.
109 Murnane, *A Million Windows,* p. 1.
110 Byron, p. 87.
111 Sontag, p. 4.
112 Ibid., p. 14.

113 Ibid., p. 8.
114 Knight, p. 3.
115 Murnane, *A History of Books*, p. 56.
116 Ibid., p. 3.
117 Ibid., p. 4.
118 Ibid., p. 83.
119 Ibid.
120 Ibid. pp. 87–8.
121 Ibid. p. 89.
122 Ibid. pp. 90, 63.
123 Murnane, 'Catherine Murnane', p. 3.
124 Ibid., p. 3.
125 Ibid., pp. 3–4.
126 Ibid. p. 4.
127 Ibid., p. 12
128 Ibid.
129 Murnane, *A History of Books*, 123.
130 Ibid. p. 81.
131 Ibid.
132 Uhlmann, 'Reporting Meaning', p. 144.
133 Murnane, *A Million Windows*, p. 11–12.
134 Ibid., p. 127.
135 Ibid., p. 153.
136 Ibid., p. 37.
137 Ibid., p. 127.
138 Ibid., p. 190.
139 Ibid., p. 30.
140 Ibid., p. 33.
141 Ibid., p. 34.
142 Ibid., p. 35.
143 Ibid.
144 Ibid., p. 15.
145 Ibid., p. 72.
146 James, *The Portrait of a Lady*, p. x.
147 Ibid., p. x.
148 Murnane, *A Season on Earth*, 187.
149 Murnane, *Border Districts*, pp. 129–30.
150 Murnane, *A Million Windows*, p. 1.
151 Ibid.
152 Ibid. p. 36.
153 Ibid. p. 1.

154 Pascal, p. 77.
155 Murnane, *Landscape with Landscape,* p. 7.
156 Murnane, *Velvet Waters,* p. 75.
157 Agamben, p. 104.
158 Kafka, p. 27.
159 Porter, p. 12.
160 Murnane, *Emerald Blue,* p. 4.
161 Murnane, *A Million Windows,* p. 31.
162 Ibid., p. 49.
163 Murnane, 'The Breathing Author', p. 165.
164 Kindt and Müller, p. 50.
165 Wimsatt and Beardsley, p. 460.
166 Booth, p. 137.
167 Ibid., p. 138.
168 Ibid., p. 74.
169 Kindt and Müller, p. 8.
170 Murnane, *Invisible Yet Enduring Lilacs,* p. i.
171 Indyk, p. 153.
172 Murnane, *Emerald Blue,* p. 215.
173 Booth, p. 265.
174 Murnane, 'The Still-Breathing Author'. p. 172.
175 Gibson, p. 119.
176 Murnane, *A Millions Windows,* p. 192.
177 Ibid., 120–21.
178 Booth, p. 159.
179 Murnane, *A Millions Windows,* p. 164.
180 James, *The Golden Bowl,* p. v.
181 Murnane, *A Millions Windows,* p. 165.
182 Ibid.
183 Ibid., p. 187.
184 Ibid., p. 183.
185 Ibid., p. 184.
186 Casey, p. 12.
187 Murnane, *A Millions Windows,* p. 146.
188 Murnane, *Border Districts,* p. 1.
189 Ibid., p. 141.
190 Ibid., p. 143.
191 Ibid.
192 Ibid., p. 10–11.
193 Bird, p. 142.
194 Heyward in Chang, n.p.

195 Murnane, *The Plains,* p. 3.
196 Murnane, *Border Districts,* p. 1.
197 Murnane in Salusinszky, p. 43.
198 Murnane, *Border Districts,* p. 11.
199 Ibid., pp. 53, 58.
200 Murnane, *The Plains,* p. 3.
201 Ibid., p. 52.
202 Ibid.
203 Ibid.
204 Ibid., pp. 51–52.
205 Ibid. p. 102.
206 See, for example, Salusinszky pp. 45–7 or Patrick West pp. 221–27.
207 Birns, *Contemporary Australian Literature*, p. 176.
208 Murnane, *The Plains,* p. 113.
209 Hassan, p. 13.
210 Murnane, *The Plains,* p. 112–13.
211 Murnane, *Border Districts,* p. 53.
212 Murnane, *The Plains,* p. 113.
213 Murnane, *Border Districts,* pp. 1–2.
214 Ibid., p. 145.
215 Ibid., p. 146.
216 Uhlmann, 'Reporting Meaning', p. 151.
217 Daniel, p. 313.
218 Murnane quoted in Macauley, p. viii.
219 Murnane, 'The Still-Breathing Author', p. 168.
220 Borges, p. 365.
221 Murnane, *Invisible Yet Enduring Lilacs,* p. 182.
222 Murnane, 'The Still-Breathing Author', p. 168.
223 Casey, p. 43.
224 Adorno, p. 123.
225 Said, p. 6.
226 Ibid., p. 8.
227 Ibid., p. 8.
228 Ibid., p. 7.
229 Tajiri, p. 80.
230 Tajiri, p. 80.
231 Murnane in Jach, n.p.
232 Dix, pp. 2–3.
233 Lorentzen, n.p.
234 Lerner, p. xi.
235 Birns, 'Reading Gerald Murnane', p. 3.

236 Phillips, 81.
237 Oakley, p. 115.
238 Casanova, p. 108.
239 Ibid., p. 108.
240 Ibid., p. 327.
241 Ibid., p. 109.
242 Genoni, p. 6.
243 Murnane, *Last Letter to a Reader,* p. 34.
244 England, p. 7.
245 Rooney, p. 69.
246 Lever, p. 229.
247 Gillet, p. 38.
248 Salusinszky, p. 30.
249 Gelder and Salzman, p. 131.
250 Mulvey, p. 17.
251 Murnane, *The Plains,* p. 95.
252 Wood, n.p.
253 Salusinszky, p. 2.
254 Ibid., p. 30.
255 Ibid.
256 Wood, n.p.
257 Ibid.
258 Murnane, *Velvet Waters,* p. 1.
259 Murnane, *Something for the Pain,* p. 128.
260 Trayhurn, p. 40.
261 Murnane, *Inland,* p. 60. This same painting—or, more specifically, the absence of the same painting—is discussed in *A History of Books* on pp. 15–17.
262 Wood, n.p.
263 Murnane, *A History of Books,* p. 14.
264 Daniel, p. 318.
265 Fry, n.p.
266 Oakley, p. 114.
267 Ibid.
268 Koval, n.p.
269 Ibid.
270 Burns, 'An Idiot', n.p.
271 Burns, 'Truth, Fiction, and True Fiction', p. 33.
272 Laxness, p. 598.
273 Murnane, *A History of Books,* p. 124.
274 Murnane, 'The Still-Breathing Author', p. 167.

Bibliography

Adorno, Theodor. *Beethoven: Philosophy of Music: Fragment and Texts.* Trans. Edmund Jephcott. Cambridge UK: Polity Press, 2019.

Agamben, Giorgio. *The Man without Content.* Trans. Georgia Albert. Stanford: Stanford UP, 1999.

Binelli, Mark. 'Is the Next Nobel Laureate in Literature Tending Bar in a Dusty Australian Town?' *The New York Times Magazine.* March 27, 2018. https://www.nytimes.com/2018/03/27/magazine/gerald-murnane-next-nobel-laureate-literature-australia.html

Bird, Carmel. 'The Murnane File: A Memoir'. *Meanjin.* Winter (2018): pp. 137–47.

Birns, Nicholas. 'Reading Gerald Murnane,' *Context* 23 (2012): pp. 3–4.

——. 'Review: *A History of Books*', *Antipodes* 27.2 (Dec 2013): pp. 222–25.

——. *Contemporary Australian Literature: A World Not Yet Dead.* Sydney: Sydney University Press, 2015.

Booth, Wayne. *The Rhetoric of Fiction,* 2nd Ed. Chicago: U. of Chicago Press, 1983.

Borges, Jorge Luis. 'Kafka and His Precursors'. *Selected Non-Fictions.* Trans. Eliot Weinberger. New York: Viking, 1999.

Burns, Shannon. "The Scientist of His Own Experience: A Profile of Gerald Murnane," *Australian Book Review,* August 2015. https://www.australianbookreview.com.au/abr-online/archive/2015/2636-the-scientist-of-his-own-experience-a-profile-of-gerald-murnane-by-shannon-burns

——. 'Gerald Murnane: An Idiot in the Greek Sense'. *Sydney Review of Books.* October 30, 2015. https://sydneyreviewofbooks.com/essay/gerald-murnane-an-idiot-in-the-greek-sense

——. 'Truth, Fiction, and True Fiction'. In *Gerald Murnane: Another World in This One*. Ed. Anthony Uhlmann. Sydney: Sydney UP, 2020, pp. 29–35.

Byron, Mark. 'Gerald Murnane's Plain Style'. In *Gerald Murnane: Another World in This One*. Ed. Anthony Uhlmann. Sydney: Sydney UP, 2020, pp. 85–106.

Casanova, Pascale. *The World Republic of Letters*. Trans. M.B. DeBevoise. Cambridge: Harvard UP, 2004.

Casey, Brendan. *The Reader of Goodwill*. [Unpublished honours thesis], University of Melbourne, 2015.

Chang, Ryan. 'Medium Making – Something About Gerald Murnane's *Border Districts*' *3:AM Magazine,* April 17, 2018. https://www.3ammagazine.com/3am/medium-making-something-gerald-murnanes-border-districts/

Coetzee, J.M. 'The Quest for Girl From Bendigo Street'. *The New York Review of Books*. 20 December 2012. https://www.nybooks.com/articles/2012/12/20/quest-girl-bendigo-street/

Craven, Peter, and Gelder, Ken. 'Criticism and Fiction in Australia'. *Overland* (Spring 2008). https://overland.org.au/feature-peter-craven-debates-ken-gelder/

Daniel, Helen. *Liars: Australian New Novelists*. Ringwood, VIC: Penguin, 1988.

Dix, Hywel, ed. *Autofiction in English*. Palgrave Macmillan, 2018.

England, Katharine. 'Post-Modern Paralysis'. *The Adelaide Advertiser*. 3 August 1985, p. 7.

Emre, Merve. *Paraliterary: The Making of Bad Readers in Postwar America*. Chicago: University of Chicago Press, 2017.

Foster, Tristan. 'Eight Questions for Gerald Murnane'. *3:AM Magazine*. April 21, 2015. https://www.3ammagazine.com/3am/eight-questions-for-gerald-murnane/

Fry, Declan. 'The Final Offering from One-of-a-Kind Writer Gerald Murnane'. *Sydney Morning Herald*. December 2, 2021. https://www.smh.com.au/culture/books/the-final-offering-from-one-of-a-kind-writer-gerald-murnane-20211129-p59d42.html

Gelder, Ken. 'Politics and Monomania'. *Overland* 184 (Spring 2006): pp. 48–56.

Gelder, Ken and Salzman, Paul. *After the Celebration: Australian Fiction 1989–2007*. Carlton, VIC: Melbourne University Publishing, 2009.

Genoni, Paul. 'The Global Reception of Post-national Literary Fiction: The Case of Gerald Murnane'. *Journal of the Association for the Study of Australian Literature*. Special Issue: Australian Literature in a Global World. (May 2009): pp. 1–13.

Gibson, Suzie. 'Landscape within Landscape: The Intertwining of the Visible and the Invisible in Gerald Murnane and Henry James'. In *Gerald Murnane: Another World in This One*. Ed. Anthony Uhlmann. Sydney: Sydney UP, 2020, pp. 107–24.

Gillet, Sue. 'Gerald Murnane's *The Plains:* A Convenient Source of Metaphors'. *Ariel: A Review of International English Literature* 26.2 (1995): pp. 25–29

Hassan, Ihab. 'Realism, Truth, and Trust in Postmodern Perspective'. *Third Text* 17.1 (2003): pp. 1–13.

Indyk, Ivor. 'What Kind of Literary History Is *A History of Books*?' In *Gerald Murnane: Another World in This One*. Ed. Anthony Uhlmann. Sydney: Sydney UP, 2020, pp. 151–62.

Jach, Antoni. 'An Interview with Gerald Murnane', *Review of Contemporary Fiction* 33.3 (Fall 2013).

James, Henry. *The Portrait of a Lady*, New York: C Scribner's Sons, 1908.

James, Henry. *The Golden Bowl*, New York: C Scribner's Sons, 1909.

Kafka, Franz. *The Collected Aphorisms*. Trans. Malcolm Pasley. New York: Penguin, 1994.

Kenner, Hugh. (1974) *A Homemade World: The American Modernist Writers*. 2nd Ed. Baltimore: Johns Hopkins UP, 1989.

Kindt, Tom and Müller, Hans-Harald. *The Implied Author: Concept and Controversy*. Berlin; New York: Walter de Gruyter, 2008.

Klee, Louis. 'Constellational Form in Gerald Murnane'. *The Cambridge Companion to the Australian Novel*. Ed. Nicholas Birns and Louis Klee. Cambridge: Cambridge UP, 2023, pp. 148–162.

Knight, Christopher. *Omissions Are Not Accidents: Modern Apophaticism from Henry James to Jacques Derrida*. Toronto: University of Toronto, 2010.

Koval, Ramona. 'The Literary Life of Gerald Murnane'. ABC Radio. 18 Feb 2008. https://www.abc.net.au/radionational/archived/bookshow/the-literary-life-of-gerald-murnane/3296040

Laxness, Halldór. *World Light*. Trans. Magnus Magnusson. New York: Vintage, 1969.

Lerner, Ben. 'The Plain Sense of Things' in Murnane, Gerald. *The Plains*, 2017, pp. vii–xiii.

Lever, Susan. 'The Cult of the Author'. *Australian Literary Studies* 16.2 (1993): p. 229. doi: 10.20314/als.b0ae88b8c5.

Lorentzen, Christian. 'Sheila Heti, Ben Lerner, Tao Lin: How "Auto" Is "Autofiction"?' *Vulture*. May 11, 2018 https://www.vulture.com/2018/05/how-auto-is-autofiction.html

Macauley, Wayne. 'Far Enough: The Peculiar World of the Plains', in Gerald Murnane, *The Plains* (Text Publishing, 2014), pp. vii–xiii.

McNamee, Brendan. *Grounded Visionary: The Mystic Fictions of Gerald Murnane.* Bern: Peter Lang, 2019.

Mulvey, Laura. 'Visual Pleasure and Narrative Cinema'. *Screen* 16.3 (October 1975), pp. 6–18.

Murnane, Gerald. (1974). *Tamarisk Row.* North Ryde, NSW: Angus and Robertson, 1977.

——. (1976) *A Lifetime on Clouds.* Ringwood, VIC: Penguin, 1989.

——. *The Plains.* Ringwood, VIC: McPhee Gribble, 1982.

——. (1985) *Landscape with Landscape.* Ringwood, VIC: Penguin, 1987.

——. *Inland.* Richmond, VIC: William Heinemann, 1988.

——. *Velvet Waters.* Ringwood, VIC: McPhee Gribble, 1990.

——. *Emerald Blue.* Ringwood, VIC: McPhee Gribble, 1995.

——. *Invisible Yet Enduring Lilacs.* Artarmon, NSW: Giramondo, 2005.

——. *Barley Patch.* Artarmon, NSW: Giramondo, 2009.

——. *A History of Books.* Artarmon, NSW: Giramondo, 2012.

——. 'The Three Archives of Gerald Murnane'. *Music and Literature* 3 (2013): pp. 16–18.

——. *A Million Windows.* Artarmon, NSW: Giramondo, 2014.

——. *Something for the Pain.* Melbourne: Text Publishing, 2015.

——. 'In Praise of the Long Sentence'. *Meanjin.* Autumn (2016): pp. 56–65.

——. 'Author's Foreword.' In *Landscape with Landscape.* Artarmon, NSW: Giramondo, 2016.

——. *Border Districts.* Artarmon, NSW: Giramondo, 2017.

——. 'The Still-Breathing Author'. *Sydney Review of Books.* February 6, 2018. https://sydneyreviewofbooks.com/essay/the-still-breathing-author-gerald-murnane/ .

——. *Green Shadows and Other Poems.* Artarmon, NSW: Giramondo, 2019.

——. *A Season on Earth.* Melbourne: Text Publishing, 2019.

——. *Last Letter to a Reader.* Artarmon, NSW: Giramondo, 2021.

Oakley, Barry. *Mug Shots: A Memoir.* Kent Town, SA: Wakefield Press, 2012.

Pascal, Blaise. (1671) *Pensées sur la Religion et sur Quelques Autres Sujets.* Samizdat, 2010.

Phillips, A.A. (1950) 'The Cultural Cringe'. In *The Words that Made Australia.* Robert Manne and Chris Feik, eds. Collingwood: Black Inc, 2012.

Porter, Hal. *The Watcher on the Cast-Iron Balcony: An Australian Autobiography.* London: Faber and Faber, 1967.

Rilke, Rainer Maria. *Letters to a Young Poet.* Trans. M.D. Herter Norton. New York: W.W.Norton, 1993.

Rooney, Brigid. 'Stream System, Salient Image and Feeling: Between *Barley Patch* and *Inland*'. In *Gerald Murnane: Another World in This One.* Ed. Anthony Uhlmann. Sydney: Sydney UP, 2020, pp. 63–84.

Said, Edward. *On Late Style: Music and Literature Against the Grain*. New York: Knopf Doubleday Publishing Group, 2007.

Salusinszky, Imre. *Gerald Murnane*. Melbourne: Oxford University Press, 1993.

Sontag, Susan. *Styles of Radical Will*. New York: Farrar, Straus and Giroux, 1966.

Steinberg, Joseph. 'Review: *Gerald Murnane: Another World in This One*'. *Journal of the Association for the Study of Australian Literature* 21.1 (2021): pp. 1–8. Retrieved at https://openjournals.library.sydney.edu.au/index.php/JASAL/article/view/15296.

——. 'Murnane's Signposts: Interview with Merve Emre'. *Sydney Review of Books*. 28 November 2022. https://sydneyreviewofbooks.com/interview/merve-emre-murnane/

Sterne, Laurence. (1767) *Tristram Shandy*. Chatham, Kent: Wordsworth Editions Ltd, 1996.

'Stream System: The Collected Short Fiction of Gerald Murnane'. *Kirkus Reviews*. 3 April 2018. https://www.kirkusreviews.com/book-reviews/gerald-murnane/stream-system/

Tajiri, Yoshiki. 'Beyond the Literary Theme Park: J. M. Coetzee's Late Style in *The Childhood of Jesus*' *Journal of Modern Literature* 39.2 (2016): pp. 74–88.

Tink, Amanda. '"Nearly all deep fertile soil": Les Murray, His Son and Autism.' *Australian Literary Studies* 37.1 (2022): doi: 10.20314/als.6d7c5d602c.

Trayhurn, Samantha, 'Images and Feelings in a Sort of Eternity": Gerald Murnane's Ideal Female Reader'. In *Gerald Murnane: Another World in This One*. Ed. Anthony Uhlmann. Sydney: Sydney UP, 2020, pp. 37–44.

Uhlmann, Anthony. 'Introduction', In *Gerald Murnane: Another World in This One*. Ed. Anthony Uhlmann. Sydney: Sydney UP, 2020, pp. 1–8.

——. 'Reporting Meaning in *Border Districts*' In *Gerald Murnane: Another World in This One*. Ed. Anthony Uhlmann. Sydney: Sydney UP, 2020, pp. 141–150.

West, Patrick. 'The Ethical Vision of Gerald Murnane'. *Journal of the Association for the Study of Australian Literature* (1996): pp. 221–27.

White, Patrick. 'The Prodigal Son'. *Australian Letters* 1.3 (April 1958): p. 39.

Wimsatt, William K. and Beardsley, Monroe. 'The Intentional Fallacy'. *The Sewanee Review* 54.3 (July–September 1946): pp. 468–88.

Windsor, Gerard. 'Flawed Fiction from a Local, Modish Messiah'. *The Bulletin*. 25 June 1985, p. 93.

Wood, Daniel Davis. 'The Purity of Potential'. *Splice*. 4 April 2018. Retrieved at https://www.thisissplice.co.uk/2018/04/04/the-purity-of-potential-gerald-murnanes-collected-short-fiction/

Acknowledgments

An earlier version of the chapter 'A Million Windows and the Implied Author' appeared as 'Remote Viewing' in *The Sydney Review of Books* in June 2014. 'The Text Ends at This Point: Border Districts' is revised from material that originally appeared in 'Retrospective Intention' from *Another World in This One* (Sydney University Press 2020). Sections from this same source on the notion of the 'implied author' have also been revised and incorporated into 'A Million Windows and the Implied Author'.

THE MIEGUNYAH PRESS

This book was designed and typeset
by Cannon Typesetting
The text was set in 11¼ point Adobe Caslon Pro
with 15½ points of leading
The text is printed on 70gsm book white
This book was edited by Catherine McInnis

THE
MIEGUNYAH
PRESS